2013, 2014, and 2015 Amendments to
the 2012 Edition of the United States

Manual for Courts-Martial

United States Government
US Army

Contents

2013 Amendments

Federal Register

Vol. 78, No. 98

Tuesday, May 21, 2013

Presidential Documents

Title 3—

The President

Executive Order 13643 of May 15, 2013

2013 Amendments to the Manual for Courts-Martial, United States

By the authority vested in me as President by the Constitution and the laws of the United States of America, including chapter 47 of title 10, United States Code (Uniform Code of Military Justice, 10 U.S.C. 801–946), and in order to prescribe amendments to the Manual for Courts-Martial, United States, prescribed by Executive Order 12473, as amended, it is hereby ordered as follows:

Section 1. Parts III and IV of the Manual for Courts-Martial, United States, are amended as described in the Annex attached and made a part of this order.

Sec. 2. These amendments shall take effect as of the date of this order, subject to the following:

(a) Nothing in these amendments shall be construed to make punishable any act done or omitted prior to the effective date of this order that was not punishable when done or omitted.

(b) Nothing in these amendments shall be construed to invalidate any nonjudicial punishment proceedings, restraint, investigation, referral of charges, trial in which arraignment occurred, or other action begun prior to the effective date of this order, and any such nonjudicial punishment, restraint, investigation, referral of charges, trial, or other action may proceed in the same manner and with the same effect as if these amendments had not been prescribed.

THE WHITE HOUSE,

May 15, 2013.

Billing code 3295–F3–P

ANNEX

Section 1. Part III of the Manual for Courts-Martial, United States, is revised to read as follows:

Rule 101. Scope

(a) *Scope.* These rules apply to court-martial proceedings to the extent and with the exceptions stated in Mil. R. Evid. 1101.

(b) *Sources of Law.* In the absence of guidance in this Manual or these rules, courts-martial will apply:

(1) first, the Federal Rules of Evidence and the case law interpreting them; and

(2) second, when not inconsistent with subdivision (b)(1), the rules of evidence at common law.

(c) *Rule of Construction.* Except as otherwise provided in these rules, the term "military judge" includes the president of a special court-martial without a military judge and a summary court-martial officer.

Rule 102. Purpose

These rules should be construed so as to administer every proceeding fairly, eliminate unjustifiable expense and delay, and promote the development of evidence law, to the end of ascertaining the truth and securing a just determination.

Rule 103. Rulings on Evidence

(a) *Preserving a Claim of Error.* A party may claim error in a ruling to admit or exclude evidence only if the error materially prejudices a substantial right of the party and:

(1) if the ruling admits evidence, a party, on the record:

(A) timely objects or moves to strike; and

(B) states the specific ground, unless it was apparent from the context; or

(2) if the ruling excludes evidence, a party informs the military judge of its substance by an offer of proof, unless the substance was apparent from the context.

(b) *Not Needing to Renew an Objection or Offer of Proof.* Once the military judge rules definitively on the record admitting or excluding evidence, either before or at trial, a party need not renew an objection or offer of proof to preserve a claim of error for appeal.

(c) *Review of Constitutional Error.* The standard provided in subdivision (a)(2) does not apply to errors implicating the United States Constitution as it applies to members of the armed forces, unless the error arises under these rules and subdivision (a)(2) provides a standard that is more advantageous to the accused than the constitutional standard.

(d) *Military Judge's Statement about the Ruling; Directing an Offer of Proof.* The military judge may make any statement about the character or form of the evidence, the objection made, and the ruling. The military judge may direct that an offer of proof be made in question-and-answer form.

(e) *Preventing the Members from Hearing Inadmissible Evidence.* In a court-martial composed of a military judge and members, to the extent practicable, the military judge must conduct a trial so that inadmissible evidence is not suggested to the members by any means.

(f) *Taking Notice of Plain Error.* A military judge may take notice of a plain error that materially prejudices a substantial right, even if the claim of error was not properly preserved.

Rule 104. Preliminary Questions

(a) *In General.* The military judge must decide any preliminary question about whether a witness is available or qualified, a privilege exists, a continuance should be granted, or evidence is admissible. In so deciding, the military judge is not bound by evidence rules, except those on privilege.

(b) *Relevance that Depends on a Fact.* When the relevance of evidence depends on whether a fact exists, proof must be introduced sufficient to support a finding that the fact does exist. The military judge may admit the proposed evidence on the condition that the proof be introduced later. A ruling on the sufficiency of evidence to support a finding of fulfillment of a condition of fact is the sole responsibility of the military judge, except where these rules or this Manual provide expressly to the contrary.

(c) *Conducting a Hearing so that the Members Cannot Hear It*. Except in cases tried before a special court-martial without a military judge, the military judge must conduct any hearing on a preliminary question so that the members cannot hear it if:

>   (1) the hearing involves the admissibility of a statement of the accused under Mil. R. Evid. 301–306;

>   (2) the accused is a witness and so requests; or

>   (3) justice so requires.

(d) *Cross-Examining the Accused*. By testifying on a preliminary question, the accused does not become subject to cross-examination on other issues in the case.

(e) *Evidence Relevant to Weight and Credibility*. This rule does not limit a party's right to introduce before the members evidence that is relevant to the weight or credibility of other evidence.

Rule 105. Limiting Evidence that Is Not Admissible against Other Parties or for Other Purposes

If the military judge admits evidence that is admissible against a party or for a purpose – but not against another party or for another purpose – the military judge, on timely request, must restrict the evidence to its proper scope and instruct the members accordingly.

Rule 106. Remainder of or Related Writings or Recorded Statements

If a party introduces all or part of a writing or recorded statement, an adverse party may require the introduction, at that time, of any other part – or any other writing or recorded statement – that in fairness ought to be considered at the same time.

Rule 201. Judicial Notice of Adjudicative Facts

(a) *Scope*. This rule governs judicial notice of an adjudicative fact only, not a legislative fact.

(b) *Kinds of Facts that May Be Judicially Noticed*. The military judge may judicially notice a fact that is not subject to reasonable dispute because it:

>   (1) is generally known universally, locally, or in the area pertinent to the event; or

>   (2) can be accurately and readily determined from sources whose accuracy cannot reasonably be questioned.

(c) *Taking Notice*. The military judge:

>   (1) may take judicial notice whether requested or not; or

>   (2) must take judicial notice if a party requests it and the military judge is supplied with the necessary information.

The military judge must inform the parties in open court when, without being requested, he or she takes judicial notice of an adjudicative fact essential to establishing an element of the case.

(d) *Timing*. The military judge may take judicial notice at any stage of the proceeding.

(e) *Opportunity to Be Heard*. On timely request, a party is entitled to be heard on the propriety of taking judicial notice and the nature of the fact to be noticed. If the military judge takes judicial notice before notifying a party, the party, on request, is still entitled to be heard.

(f) *Instructing the Members*. The military judge must instruct the members that they may or may not accept the noticed fact as conclusive.

Rule 202. Judicial Notice of Law

(a) *Domestic Law*. The military judge may take judicial notice of domestic law. If a domestic law is a fact that is of consequence to the determination of the action, the procedural requirements of Mil. R. Evid. 201 – except Rule 201(f) – apply.

(b) *Foreign Law*. A party who intends to raise an issue concerning the law of a foreign country must give reasonable written notice. The military judge, in determining foreign law, may consider any relevant material or source, in accordance with Mil. R. Evid. 104. Such a determination is a ruling on a question of law.

Rule 301. Privilege Concerning Compulsory Self-Incrimination

(a) *General Rule*. An individual may claim the most favorable privilege provided by the Fifth Amendment to the United States Constitution, Article 31, or these rules. The privileges against self-incrimination are applicable only to evidence of a testimonial or communicative nature.

2

(b) *Standing*. The privilege of a witness to refuse to respond to a question that may tend to incriminate the witness is a personal one that the witness may exercise or waive at his or her discretion.

(c) *Limited Waiver*. An accused who chooses to testify as a witness waives the privilege against self-incrimination only with respect to the matters about which he or she testifies. If the accused is on trial for two or more offenses and on direct examination testifies about only one or some of the offenses, the accused may not be cross-examined as to guilt or innocence with respect to the other offenses unless the cross-examination is relevant to an offense concerning which the accused has testified. This waiver is subject to Mil. R. Evid. 608(b).

(d) *Exercise of the Privilege*. If a witness states that the answer to a question may tend to incriminate him or her, the witness cannot be required to answer unless the military judge finds that the facts and circumstances are such that no answer the witness might make to the question would tend to incriminate the witness or that the witness has, with respect to the question, waived the privilege against self-incrimination. A witness may not assert the privilege if he or she is not subject to criminal penalty as a result of an answer by reason of immunity, running of the statute of limitations, or similar reason.

    (1) *Immunity Requirements*. The minimum grant of immunity adequate to overcome the privilege is that which under either R.C.M. 704 or other proper authority provides that neither the testimony of the witness nor any evidence obtained from that testimony may be used against the witness at any subsequent trial other than in a prosecution for perjury, false swearing, the making of a false official statement, or failure to comply with an order to testify after the military judge has ruled that the privilege may not be asserted by reason of immunity.

    (2) *Notification of Immunity or Leniency*. When a prosecution witness before a court-martial has been granted immunity or leniency in exchange for testimony, the grant must be reduced to writing and must be served on the accused prior to arraignment or within a reasonable time before the witness testifies. If notification is not made as required by this rule, the military judge may grant a continuance until notification is made, prohibit or strike the testimony of the witness, or enter such other order as may be required.

(e) *Waiver of the Privilege*. A witness who answers a self-incriminating question without having asserted the privilege against self-incrimination may be required to answer questions relevant to the disclosure, unless the questions are likely to elicit additional self-incriminating information.

    (1) If a witness asserts the privilege against self-incrimination on cross-examination, the military judge, upon motion, may strike the direct testimony of the witness in whole or in part, unless the matters to which the witness refuses to testify are purely collateral.

    (2) Any limited waiver of the privilege under subdivision (e) applies only at the trial in which the answer is given, does not extend to a rehearing or new or other trial, and is subject to Mil. R. Evid. 608(b).

(f) *Effect of Claiming the Privilege*.

    (1) *No Inference to Be Drawn*. The fact that a witness has asserted the privilege against self-incrimination cannot be considered as raising any inference unfavorable to either the accused or the government.

    (2) *Pretrial Invocation Not Admissible*. The fact that the accused during official questioning and in exercise of rights under the Fifth Amendment to the United States Constitution or Article 31 remained silent, refused to answer a certain question, requested counsel, or requested that the questioning be terminated, is not admissible against the accused.

    (3) *Instructions Regarding the Privilege*. When the accused does not testify at trial, defense counsel may request that the members of the court be instructed to disregard that fact and not to draw any adverse inference from it. Defense counsel may request that the members not be so instructed. Defense counsel's election will be binding upon the military judge except that the military judge may give the instruction when the instruction is necessary in the interests of justice.

Rule 302. Privilege Concerning Mental Examination of an Accused

(a) *General Rule*. The accused has a privilege to prevent any statement made by the accused at a mental examination ordered under R.C.M. 706 and any derivative evidence obtained through use of such a statement from being received into evidence against the accused on the issue of guilt or innocence or during sentencing proceedings. This privilege may be claimed by the accused notwithstanding the fact that the accused may have been warned of the rights provided by Mil. R. Evid. 305 at the examination.

(b) *Exceptions*.

    (1) There is no privilege under this rule when the accused first introduces into evidence such statements or derivative evidence.

(2) If the court-martial has allowed the defense to present expert testimony as to the mental condition of the accused, an expert witness for the prosecution may testify as to the reasons for his or her conclusions, but such testimony may not extend to statements of the accused except as provided in subdivision (b)(1).

(c) *Release of Evidence from an R.C.M. 706 Examination*. If the defense offers expert testimony concerning the mental condition of the accused, the military judge, upon motion, must order the release to the prosecution of the full contents, other than any statements made by the accused, of any report prepared pursuant to R.C.M. 706. If the defense offers statements made by the accused at such examination, the military judge, upon motion, may order the disclosure of such statements made by the accused and contained in the report as may be necessary in the interests of justice.

(d) *Noncompliance by the Accused*. The military judge may prohibit an accused who refuses to cooperate in a mental examination authorized under R.C.M. 706 from presenting any expert medical testimony as to any issue that would have been the subject of the mental examination.

(e) *Procedure*. The privilege in this rule may be claimed by the accused only under the procedure set forth in Mil. R. Evid. 304 for an objection or a motion to suppress.

Rule 303. Degrading Questions

Statements and evidence are inadmissible if they are not material to the issue and may tend to degrade the person testifying.

Rule 304. Confessions and Admissions

(a) *General Rule*. If the accused makes a timely motion or objection under this rule, an involuntary statement from the accused, or any evidence derived therefrom, is inadmissible at trial except as provided in subdivision (e).

   (1) *Definitions*. As used in this rule:

      (A) "Involuntary statement" means a statement obtained in violation of the self-incrimination privilege or Due Process Clause of the Fifth Amendment to the United States Constitution, Article 31, or through the use of coercion, unlawful influence, or unlawful inducement.

      (B) "Confession" means an acknowledgment of guilt.

      (C) "Admission" means a self-incriminating statement falling short of an acknowledgment of guilt, even if it was intended by its maker to be exculpatory.

   (2) Failure to deny an accusation of wrongdoing is not an admission of the truth of the accusation if at the time of the alleged failure the person was under investigation or was in confinement, arrest, or custody for the alleged wrongdoing.

(b) *Evidence Derived from a Statement of the Accused*. When the defense has made an appropriate and timely motion or objection under this rule, evidence allegedly derived from a statement of the accused may not be admitted unless the military judge finds by a preponderance of the evidence that:

   (1) the statement was made voluntarily,

   (2) the evidence was not obtained by use of the accused's statement, or

   (3) the evidence would have been obtained even if the statement had not been made.

(c) *Corroboration of a Confession or Admission*.

   (1) An admission or a confession of the accused may be considered as evidence against the accused on the question of guilt or innocence only if independent evidence, either direct or circumstantial, has been admitted into evidence that corroborates the essential facts admitted to justify sufficiently an inference of their truth.

   (2) Other uncorroborated confessions or admissions of the accused that would themselves require corroboration may not be used to supply this independent evidence. If the independent evidence raises an inference of the truth of some but not all of the essential facts admitted, then the confession or admission may be considered as evidence against the accused only with respect to those essential facts stated in the confession or admission that are corroborated by the independent evidence.

   (3) Corroboration is not required for a statement made by the accused before the court by which the accused is being tried, for statements made prior to or contemporaneously with the act, or for statements offered under a rule of evidence other than that pertaining to the admissibility of admissions or confessions.

   (4) *Quantum of Evidence Needed*. The independent evidence necessary to establish corroboration need not be sufficient of itself to establish beyond a reasonable doubt the truth of facts stated in the admission or confession. The independent evidence need raise only an inference of the truth of the essential facts admitted. The amount and type

4

of evidence introduced as corroboration is a factor to be considered by the trier of fact in determining the weight, if any, to be given to the admission or confession.

(5) *Procedure.* The military judge alone is to determine when adequate evidence of corroboration has been received. Corroborating evidence must be introduced before the admission or confession is introduced unless the military judge allows submission of such evidence subject to later corroboration.

(d) *Disclosure of Statements by the Accused and Derivative Evidence.* Before arraignment, the prosecution must disclose to the defense the contents of all statements, oral or written, made by the accused that are relevant to the case, known to the trial counsel, and within the control of the armed forces, and all evidence derived from such statements, that the prosecution intends to offer against the accused.

(e) *Limited Use of an Involuntary Statement.* A statement obtained in violation of Article 31 or Mil. R. Evid. 305(b)-(c) may be used only:

(1) to impeach by contradiction the in-court testimony of the accused; or

(2) in a later prosecution against the accused for perjury, false swearing, or the making of a false official statement.

(f) *Motions and Objections.*

(1) Motions to suppress or objections under this rule, or Mil. R. Evid. 302 or 305, to any statement or derivative evidence that has been disclosed must be made by the defense prior to submission of a plea. In the absence of such motion or objection, the defense may not raise the issue at a later time except as permitted by the military judge for good cause shown. Failure to so move or object constitutes a waiver of the objection.

(2) If the prosecution seeks to offer a statement made by the accused or derivative evidence that was not disclosed before arraignment, the prosecution must provide timely notice to the military judge and defense counsel. The defense may object at that time and the military judge may make such orders as are required in the interests of justice.

(3) The defense may present evidence relevant to the admissibility of evidence as to which there has been an objection or motion to suppress under this rule. An accused may testify for the limited purpose of denying that the accused made the statement or that the statement was made voluntarily.

(A) Prior to the introduction of such testimony by the accused, the defense must inform the military judge that the testimony is offered under subdivision (f)(3).

(B) When the accused testifies under subdivision (f)(3), the accused may be cross-examined only as to the matter on which he or she testifies. Nothing said by the accused on either direct or cross-examination may be used against the accused for any purpose other than in a prosecution for perjury, false swearing, or the making of a false official statement.

(4) *Specificity.* The military judge may require the defense to specify the grounds upon which the defense moves to suppress or object to evidence. If defense counsel, despite the exercise of due diligence, has been unable to interview adequately those persons involved in the taking of a statement, the military judge may make any order required in the interests of justice, including authorization for the defense to make a general motion to suppress or general objection.

(5) *Rulings.* The military judge must rule, prior to plea, upon any motion to suppress or objection to evidence made prior to plea unless, for good cause, the military judge orders that the ruling be deferred for determination at trial or after findings. The military judge may not defer ruling if doing so adversely affects a party's right to appeal the ruling. The military judge must state essential findings of fact on the record when the ruling involves factual issues.

(6) *Burden of Proof.* When the defense has made an appropriate motion or objection under this rule, the prosecution has the burden of establishing the admissibility of the evidence. When the military judge has required a specific motion or objection under subdivision (f)(4), the burden on the prosecution extends only to the grounds upon which the defense moved to suppress or object to the evidence.

(7) *Standard of Proof.* The military judge must find by a preponderance of the evidence that a statement by the accused was made voluntarily before it may be received into evidence. When trial is by a special court-martial without a military judge, a determination by the president of the court that a statement was made voluntarily is subject to objection by any member of the court. When such objection is made, it will be resolved pursuant to R.C.M. 801(e)(3)(C).

(8) *Effect of Guilty Plea.* Except as otherwise expressly provided in R.C.M. 910(a)(2), a plea of guilty to an offense that results in a finding of guilty waives all privileges against self-incrimination and all motions and objections under this rule with respect to that offense regardless of whether raised prior to plea.

5

(g) *Weight of the Evidence.* If a statement is admitted into evidence, the military judge must permit the defense to present relevant evidence with respect to the voluntariness of the statement and must instruct the members to give such weight to the statement as it deserves under all the circumstances.

(h) *Completeness.* If only part of an alleged admission or confession is introduced against the accused, the defense, by cross-examination or otherwise, may introduce the remaining portions of the statement.

(i) *Evidence of an Oral Statement.* A voluntary oral confession or admission of the accused may be proved by the testimony of anyone who heard the accused make it, even if it was reduced to writing and the writing is not accounted for.

(j) *Refusal to Obey an Order to Submit a Body Substance.* If an accused refuses a lawful order to submit for chemical analysis a sample of his or her blood, breath, urine or other body substance, evidence of such refusal may be admitted into evidence on:

(1) a charge of violating an order to submit such a sample; or

(2) any other charge on which the results of the chemical analysis would have been admissible.

Rule 305. Warnings about Rights

(a) *General Rule.* A statement obtained in violation of this rule is involuntary and will be treated under Mil. R. Evid. 304.

(b) *Definitions.* As used in this rule:

(1) "Person subject to the code" means a person subject to the Uniform Code of Military Justice as contained in Chapter 47 of Title 10, United States Code. This term includes, for purposes of subdivision (c) of this rule, a knowing agent of any such person or of a military unit.

(2) "Interrogation" means any formal or informal questioning in which an incriminating response either is sought or is a reasonable consequence of such questioning.

(3) "Custodial interrogation" means questioning that takes place while the accused or suspect is in custody, could reasonably believe himself or herself to be in custody, or is otherwise deprived of his or her freedom of action in any significant way.

(c) *Warnings Concerning the Accusation, Right to Remain Silent, and Use of Statements.*

(1) *Article 31 Rights Warnings.* A statement obtained from the accused in violation of the accused's rights under Article 31 is involuntary and therefore inadmissible against the accused except as provided in subdivision (d). Pursuant to Article 31, a person subject to the code may not interrogate or request any statement from an accused or a person suspected of an offense without first:

(A) informing the accused or suspect of the nature of the accusation;

(B) advising the accused or suspect that the accused or suspect has the right to remain silent; and

(C) advising the accused or suspect that any statement made may be used as evidence against the accused or suspect in a trial by court-martial.

(2) *Fifth Amendment Right to Counsel.* If a person suspected of an offense and subjected to custodial interrogation requests counsel, any statement made in the interrogation after such request, or evidence derived from the interrogation after such request, is inadmissible against the accused unless counsel was present for the interrogation.

(3) *Sixth Amendment Right to Counsel.* If an accused against whom charges have been preferred is interrogated on matters concerning the preferred charges by anyone acting in a law enforcement capacity, or the agent of such a person, and the accused requests counsel, or if the accused has appointed or retained counsel, any statement made in the interrogation, or evidence derived from the interrogation, is inadmissible unless counsel was present for the interrogation.

(4) *Exercise of Rights.* If a person chooses to exercise the privilege against self-incrimination, questioning must cease immediately. If a person who is subjected to interrogation under the circumstances described in subdivisions (c)(2) or (c)(3) of this rule chooses to exercise the right to counsel, questioning must cease until counsel is present.

(d) *Presence of Counsel.* When a person entitled to counsel under this rule requests counsel, a judge advocate or an individual certified in accordance with Article 27(b) will be provided by the United States at no expense to the person and without regard to the person's indigency and must be present before the interrogation may proceed. In addition to counsel supplied by the United States, the person may retain civilian counsel at no expense to the United States. Unless otherwise provided by regulations of the Secretary concerned, an accused or suspect does not have a right under this rule to have military counsel of his or her own selection.

6

(e) *Waiver.*

(1) *Waiver of the Privilege Against Self-Incrimination.* After receiving applicable warnings under this rule, a person may waive the rights described therein and in Mil. R. Evid. 301 and make a statement. The waiver must be made freely, knowingly, and intelligently. A written waiver is not required. The accused or suspect must affirmatively acknowledge that he or she understands the rights involved, affirmatively decline the right to counsel, and affirmatively consent to making a statement.

(2) *Waiver of the Right to Counsel.* If the right to counsel is applicable under this rule and the accused or suspect does not affirmatively decline the right to counsel, the prosecution must demonstrate by a preponderance of the evidence that the individual waived the right to counsel.

(3) *Waiver After Initially Invoking the Right to Counsel.*

(A) *Fifth Amendment Right to Counsel.* If an accused or suspect subjected to custodial interrogation requests counsel, any subsequent waiver of the right to counsel obtained during a custodial interrogation concerning the same or different offenses is invalid unless the prosecution can demonstrate by a preponderance of the evidence that:

(i) the accused or suspect initiated the communication leading to the waiver; or

(ii) the accused or suspect has not continuously had his or her freedom restricted by confinement, or other means, during the period between the request for counsel and the subsequent waiver.

(B) *Sixth Amendment Right to Counsel.* If an accused or suspect interrogated after preferral of charges as described in subdivision (c)(1) requests counsel, any subsequent waiver of the right to counsel obtained during an interrogation concerning the same offenses is invalid unless the prosecution can demonstrate by a preponderance of the evidence that the accused or suspect initiated the communication leading to the waiver.

(f) *Standards for Nonmilitary Interrogations.*

(1) *United States Civilian Interrogations.* When a person subject to the code is interrogated by an official or agent of the United States, of the District of Columbia, or of a State, Commonwealth, or possession of the United States, or any political subdivision of such a State, Commonwealth, or possession, the person's entitlement to rights warnings and the validity of any waiver of applicable rights will be determined by the principles of law generally recognized in the trial of criminal cases in the United States district courts involving similar interrogations.

(2) *Foreign Interrogations.* Warnings under Article 31 and the Fifth and Sixth Amendments to the United States Constitution are not required during an interrogation conducted outside of a State, district, Commonwealth, territory, or possession of the United States by officials of a foreign government or their agents unless such interrogation is conducted, instigated, or participated in by military personnel or their agents or by those officials or agents listed in subdivision (f)(1). A statement obtained from a foreign interrogation is admissible unless the statement is obtained through the use of coercion, unlawful influence, or unlawful inducement. An interrogation is not "participated in" by military personnel or their agents or by the officials or agents listed in subdivision (f)(1) merely because such a person was present at an interrogation conducted in a foreign nation by officials of a foreign government or their agents, or because such a person acted as an interpreter or took steps to mitigate damage to property or physical harm during the foreign interrogation.

Rule 306. Statements by One of Several Accused

When two or more accused are tried at the same trial, evidence of a statement made by one of them which is admissible only against him or her or only against some but not all of the accused may not be received in evidence unless all references inculpating an accused against whom the statement is inadmissible are deleted effectively or the maker of the statement is subject to cross-examination.

Rule 311. Evidence Obtained from Unlawful Searches and Seizures

(a) *General Rule.* Evidence obtained as a result of an unlawful search or seizure made by a person acting in a governmental capacity is inadmissible against the accused if:

(1) the accused makes a timely motion to suppress or an objection to the evidence under this rule; and

(2) the accused had a reasonable expectation of privacy in the person, place or property searched; the accused had a legitimate interest in the property or evidence seized when challenging a seizure; or the accused would otherwise have grounds to object to the search or seizure under the Constitution of the United States as applied to members of the armed forces.

(b) *Definition.* As used in this rule, a search or seizure is "unlawful" if it was conducted, instigated, or participated in by:

7

(1) military personnel or their agents and was in violation of the Constitution of the United States as applied to members of the armed forces, a federal statute applicable to trials by court-martial that requires exclusion of evidence obtained in violation thereof, or Mil. R. Evid. 312–317;

(2) other officials or agents of the United States, of the District of Columbia, or of a State, Commonwealth, or possession of the United States or any political subdivision of such a State, Commonwealth, or possession, and was in violation of the Constitution of the United States, or is unlawful under the principles of law generally applied in the trial of criminal cases in the United States district courts involving a similar search or seizure; or

(3) officials of a foreign government or their agents, where evidence was obtained as a result of a foreign search or seizure that subjected the accused to gross and brutal maltreatment. A search or seizure is not "participated in" by a United States military or civilian official merely because that person is present at a search or seizure conducted in a foreign nation by officials of a foreign government or their agents, or because that person acted as an interpreter or took steps to mitigate damage to property or physical harm during the foreign search or seizure.

(c) *Exceptions.*

(1) *Impeachment.* Evidence that was obtained as a result of an unlawful search or seizure may be used to impeach by contradiction the in-court testimony of the accused.

(2) *Inevitable Discovery.* Evidence that was obtained as a result of an unlawful search or seizure may be used when the evidence would have been obtained even if such unlawful search or seizure had not been made.

(3) *Good Faith Execution of a Warrant or Search Authorization.* Evidence that was obtained as a result of an unlawful search or seizure may be used if:

(A) the search or seizure resulted from an authorization to search, seize or apprehend issued by an individual competent to issue the authorization under Mil. R. Evid. 315(d) or from a search warrant or arrest warrant issued by competent civilian authority;

(B) the individual issuing the authorization or warrant had a substantial basis for determining the existence of probable cause; and

(C) the officials seeking and executing the authorization or warrant reasonably and with good faith relied on the issuance of the authorization or warrant. Good faith is to be determined using an objective standard.

(d) *Motions to Suppress and Objections.*

(1) *Disclosure.* Prior to arraignment, the prosecution must disclose to the defense all evidence seized from the person or property of the accused, or believed to be owned by the accused, or evidence derived therefrom, that it intends to offer into evidence against the accused at trial.

(2) *Time Requirements.*

(A) When evidence has been disclosed prior to arraignment under subdivision (d)(1), the defense must make any motion to suppress or objection under this rule prior to submission of a plea. In the absence of such motion or objection, the defense may not raise the issue at a later time except as permitted by the military judge for good cause shown. Failure to so move or object constitutes a waiver of the motion or objection.

(B) If the prosecution intends to offer evidence described in subdivision (d)(1) that was not disclosed prior to arraignment, the prosecution must provide timely notice to the military judge and to counsel for the accused. The defense may enter an objection at that time and the military judge may make such orders as are required in the interest of justice.

(3) *Specificity.* The military judge may require the defense to specify the grounds upon which the defense moves to suppress or object to evidence described in subdivision (d)(1). If defense counsel, despite the exercise of due diligence, has been unable to interview adequately those persons involved in the search or seizure, the military judge may enter any order required by the interests of justice, including authorization for the defense to make a general motion to suppress or a general objection.

(4) *Challenging Probable Cause.*

(A) *Relevant Evidence.* If the defense challenges evidence seized pursuant to a search warrant or search authorization on the ground that the warrant or authorization was not based upon probable cause, the evidence relevant to the motion is limited to evidence concerning the information actually presented to or otherwise known by the authorizing officer, except as provided in subdivision (d)(4)(B).

(B) *False Statements.* If the defense makes a substantial preliminary showing that a government agent included a false statement knowingly and intentionally or with reckless disregard for the truth in the information presented to the authorizing officer, and if the allegedly false statement is necessary to the finding of probable cause, the defense, upon request, is entitled to a hearing. At the hearing, the defense has the burden of establishing by a preponderance of the evidence the allegation of knowing and intentional falsity or reckless disregard for the truth. If

8

the defense meets its burden, the prosecution has the burden of proving by a preponderance of the evidence, with the false information set aside, that the remaining information presented to the authorizing officer is sufficient to establish probable cause. If the prosecution does not meet its burden, the objection or motion must be granted unless the search is otherwise lawful under these rules.

(5) *Burden and Standard of Proof.*

(A) *In general.* When the defense makes an appropriate motion or objection under subdivision (d), the prosecution has the burden of proving by a preponderance of the evidence that the evidence was not obtained as a result of an unlawful search or seizure, that the evidence would have been obtained even if the unlawful search or seizure had not been made, or that the evidence was obtained by officials who reasonably and with good faith relied on the issuance of an authorization to search, seize, or apprehend or a search warrant or an arrest warrant.

(B) *Statement Following Apprehension.* In addition to subdivision (d)(5)(A), a statement obtained from a person apprehended in a dwelling in violation R.C.M. 302(d)(2) and (e), is admissible if the prosecution shows by a preponderance of the evidence that the apprehension was based on probable cause, the statement was made at a location outside the dwelling subsequent to the apprehension, and the statement was otherwise in compliance with these rules.

(C) *Specific Grounds of Motion or Objection.* When the military judge has required the defense to make a specific motion or objection under subdivision (d)(3), the burden on the prosecution extends only to the grounds upon which the defense moved to suppress or objected to the evidence.

(6) *Defense Evidence.* The defense may present evidence relevant to the admissibility of evidence as to which there has been an appropriate motion or objection under this rule. An accused may testify for the limited purpose of contesting the legality of the search or seizure giving rise to the challenged evidence. Prior to the introduction of such testimony by the accused, the defense must inform the military judge that the testimony is offered under subdivision (d). When the accused testifies under subdivision (d), the accused may be cross-examined only as to the matter on which he or she testifies. Nothing said by the accused on either direct or cross-examination may be used against the accused for any purpose other than in a prosecution for perjury, false swearing, or the making of a false official statement.

(7) *Rulings.* The military judge must rule, prior to plea, upon any motion to suppress or objection to evidence made prior to plea unless, for good cause, the military judge orders that the ruling be deferred for determination at trial or after findings. The military judge may not defer ruling if doing so adversely affects a party's right to appeal the ruling. The military judge must state essential findings of fact on the record when the ruling involves factual issues.

(8) *Informing the Members.* If a defense motion or objection under this rule is sustained in whole or in part, the court-martial members may not be informed of that fact except when the military judge must instruct the members to disregard evidence.

(e) *Effect of Guilty Plea.* Except as otherwise expressly provided in R.C.M. 910(a)(2), a plea of guilty to an offense that results in a finding of guilty waives all issues under the Fourth Amendment to the Constitution of the United States and Mil. R. Evid. 311-317 with respect to the offense, whether or not raised prior to plea.

Rule 312. Body Views and Intrusions

(a) *General Rule.* Evidence obtained from body views and intrusions conducted in accordance with this rule is admissible at trial when relevant and not otherwise inadmissible under these rules.

(b) *Visual Examination of the Body.*

(1) *Consensual Examination.* Evidence obtained from a visual examination of the unclothed body is admissible if the person consented to the inspection in accordance with Mil. R. Evid. 314(e).

(2) *Involuntary Examination.* Evidence obtained from an involuntary display of the unclothed body, including a visual examination of body cavities, is admissible only if the inspection was conducted in a reasonable fashion and authorized under the following provisions of the Military Rules of Evidence:

(A) inspections and inventories under Mil. R. Evid. 313;

(B) searches under Mil. R. Evid. 314(b) and 314(c) if there is a reasonable suspicion that weapons, contraband, or evidence of crime is concealed on the body of the person to be searched;

(C) searches incident to lawful apprehension under Mil. R. Evid. 314(g);

(D) searches within a jail, confinement facility, or similar facility under Mil. R. Evid. 314(h) if reasonably necessary to maintain the security of the institution or its personnel;

(E) emergency searches under Mil. R. Evid. 314(i); and

9

(F) probable cause searches under Mil. R. Evid. 315.

(c) *Intrusion into Body Cavities.*

(1) *Mouth, Nose, and Ears.* Evidence obtained from a reasonable nonconsensual physical intrusion into the mouth, nose, and ears is admissible under the same standards that apply to a visual examination of the body under subdivision (b).

(2) *Other Body Cavities.* Evidence obtained from nonconsensual intrusions into other body cavities is admissible only if made in a reasonable fashion by a person with appropriate medical qualifications and if:

(A) at the time of the intrusion there was probable cause to believe that a weapon, contraband, or other evidence of crime was present;

(B) conducted to remove weapons, contraband, or evidence of crime discovered under subdivisions (b) or (c)(2)(A) of this rule;

(C) conducted pursuant to Mil. R. Evid. 316(c)(5)(C);

(D) conducted pursuant to a search warrant or search authorization under Mil. R. Evid. 315; or

(E) conducted pursuant to Mil. R. Evid. 314(h) based on a reasonable suspicion that the individual is concealing a weapon, contraband, or evidence of crime.

(d) *Extraction of Body Fluids.* Evidence obtained from nonconsensual extraction of body fluids is admissible if seized pursuant to a search warrant or a search authorization under Mil. R. Evid. 315. Evidence obtained from nonconsensual extraction of body fluids made without such a warrant or authorization is admissible, notwithstanding Mil. R. Evid. 315(g), only when probable cause existed at the time of extraction to believe that evidence of crime would be found and that the delay necessary to obtain a search warrant or search authorization could have resulted in the destruction of the evidence. Evidence obtained from nonconsensual extraction of body fluids is admissible only when executed in a reasonable fashion by a person with appropriate medical qualifications.

(e) *Other Intrusive Searches.* Evidence obtained from a nonconsensual intrusive search of the body, other than searches described in subdivisions (c) or (d), conducted to locate or obtain weapons, contraband, or evidence of crime is admissible only if obtained pursuant to a search warrant or search authorization under Mil. R. Evid. 315 and conducted in a reasonable fashion by a person with appropriate medical qualifications in such a manner so as not to endanger the health of the person to be searched.

(f) *Intrusions for Valid Medical Purposes.* Evidence or contraband obtained in the course of a medical examination or an intrusion conducted for a valid medical purpose is admissible. Such an examination or intrusion may not, for the purpose of obtaining evidence or contraband, exceed what is necessary for the medical purpose.

(g) *Medical Qualifications.* The Secretary concerned may prescribe appropriate medical qualifications for persons who conduct searches and seizures under this rule.

Rule 313. Inspections and Inventories in the Armed Forces

(a) *General Rule.* Evidence obtained from lawful inspections and inventories in the armed forces is admissible at trial when relevant and not otherwise inadmissible under these rules. An unlawful weapon, contraband, or other evidence of a crime discovered during a lawful inspection or inventory may be seized and is admissible in accordance with this rule.

(b) *Lawful Inspections.* An "inspection" is an examination of the whole or part of a unit, organization, installation, vessel, aircraft, or vehicle, including an examination conducted at entrance and exit points, conducted as an incident of command the primary purpose of which is to determine and to ensure the security, military fitness, or good order and discipline of the unit, organization, installation, vessel, aircraft, or vehicle. Inspections must be conducted in a reasonable fashion and, if applicable, must comply with Mil. R. Evid. 312. Inspections may utilize any reasonable natural or technological aid and may be conducted with or without notice to those inspected.

(1) *Purpose of Inspections.* An inspection may include, but is not limited to, an examination to determine and to ensure that any or all of the following requirements are met: that the command is properly equipped, functioning properly, maintaining proper standards of readiness, sea or airworthiness, sanitation and cleanliness; and that personnel are present, fit, and ready for duty. An order to produce body fluids, such as urine, is permissible in accordance with this rule.

(2) *Searches for Evidence.* An examination made for the primary purpose of obtaining evidence for use in a trial by court-martial or in other disciplinary proceedings is not an inspection within the meaning of this rule.

(3) *Examinations to Locate and Confiscate Weapons or Contraband.*

(A) An inspection may include an examination to locate and confiscate unlawful weapons and other contraband provided that the criteria set forth in subdivision (b)(3)(B) are not implicated.

10

(B) The prosecution must prove by clear and convincing evidence that the examination was an inspection within the meaning of this rule if a purpose of an examination is to locate weapons or contraband, and if:

(i) the examination was directed immediately following a report of a specific offense in the unit, organization, installation, vessel, aircraft, or vehicle and was not previously scheduled;

(ii) specific individuals are selected for examination; or

(iii) persons examined are subjected to substantially different intrusions during the same examination.

(c) *Lawful Inventories.* An "inventory" is a reasonable examination, accounting, or other control measure used to account for or control property, assets, or other resources. It is administrative and not prosecutorial in nature, and if applicable, the inventory must comply with Mil. R. Evid. 312. An examination made for the primary purpose of obtaining evidence for use in a trial by court-martial or in other disciplinary proceedings is not an inventory within the meaning of this rule.

Rule 314. Searches Not Requiring Probable Cause

(a) *General Rule.* Evidence obtained from reasonable searches not requiring probable cause is admissible at trial when relevant and not otherwise inadmissible under these rules or the Constitution of the United States as applied to members of the armed forces.

(b) *Border Searches.* Evidence from a border search for customs or immigration purposes authorized by a federal statute is admissible.

(c) *Searches Upon Entry to or Exit from United States Installations, Aircraft, and Vessels Abroad.* In addition to inspections under Mil. R. Evid. 313(b), evidence is admissible when a commander of a United States military installation, enclave, or aircraft on foreign soil, or in foreign or international airspace, or a United States vessel in foreign or international waters, has authorized appropriate personnel to search persons or the property of such persons upon entry to or exit from the installation, enclave, aircraft, or vessel to ensure the security, military fitness, or good order and discipline of the command. A search made for the primary purpose of obtaining evidence for use in a trial by court-martial or other disciplinary proceeding is not authorized by subdivision (c).

(d) *Searches of Government Property.* Evidence resulting from a search of government property without probable cause is admissible under this rule unless the person to whom the property is issued or assigned has a reasonable expectation of privacy therein at the time of the search. Normally a person does not have a reasonable expectation of privacy in government property that is not issued for personal use. Wall or floor lockers in living quarters issued for the purpose of storing personal possessions normally are issued for personal use, but the determination as to whether a person has a reasonable expectation of privacy in government property issued for personal use depends on the facts and circumstances at the time of the search.

(e) *Consent Searches.*

(1) *General Rule.* Evidence of a search conducted without probable cause is admissible if conducted with lawful consent.

(2) *Who May Consent.* A person may consent to a search of his or her person or property, or both, unless control over such property has been given to another. A person may grant consent to search property when the person exercises control over that property.

(3) *Scope of Consent.* Consent may be limited in any way by the person granting consent, including limitations in terms of time, place, or property, and may be withdrawn at any time.

(4) *Voluntariness.* To be valid, consent must be given voluntarily. Voluntariness is a question to be determined from all the circumstances. Although a person's knowledge of the right to refuse to give consent is a factor to be considered in determining voluntariness, the prosecution is not required to demonstrate such knowledge as a prerequisite to establishing a voluntary consent. Mere submission to the color of authority of personnel performing law enforcement duties or acquiescence in an announced or indicated purpose to search is not a voluntary consent.

(5) *Burden and Standard of Proof.* The prosecution must prove consent by clear and convincing evidence. The fact that a person was in custody while granting consent is a factor to be considered in determining the voluntariness of consent, but it does not affect the standard of proof.

(f) *Searches Incident to a Lawful Stop.*

(1) *Lawfulness.* A stop is lawful when conducted by a person authorized to apprehend under R.C.M. 302(b) or others performing law enforcement duties and when the person making the stop has information or observes unusual conduct that leads him or her reasonably to conclude in light of his or her experience that criminal activity may be afoot. The stop must be temporary and investigatory in nature.

11

(2) *Stop and Frisk.* Evidence is admissible if seized from a person who was lawfully stopped and who was frisked for weapons because he or she was reasonably suspected to be armed and dangerous. Contraband or evidence that is located in the process of a lawful frisk may be seized.

(3) *Vehicles.* Evidence is admissible if seized in the course of a search for weapons in the areas of the passenger compartment of a vehicle in which a weapon may be placed or hidden, so long as the person lawfully stopped is the driver or a passenger and the official who made the stop has a reasonable suspicion that the person stopped is dangerous and may gain immediate control of a weapon.

(g) *Searches Incident to Apprehension.*

(1) *General Rule.* Evidence is admissible if seized in a search of a person who has been lawfully apprehended or if seized as a result of a reasonable protective sweep.

(2) *Search for Weapons and Destructible Evidence.* A lawful search incident to apprehension may include a search for weapons or destructible evidence in the area within the immediate control of a person who has been apprehended. "Immediate control" means that area in which the individual searching could reasonably believe that the person apprehended could reach with a sudden movement to obtain such property.

(3) *Protective Sweep for Other Persons.*

(A) *Area of Potential Immediate Attack.* Apprehending officials may, incident to apprehension, as a precautionary matter and without probable cause or reasonable suspicion, look in closets and other spaces immediately adjoining the place of apprehension from which an attack could be immediately launched.

(B) *Wider Protective Sweep.* When an apprehension takes place at a location in which another person might be present who might endanger the apprehending officials or others in the area of the apprehension, a search incident to arrest may lawfully include a reasonable examination of those spaces where a person might be found. Such a reasonable examination is lawful under subdivision (g) if the apprehending official has a reasonable suspicion based on specific and articulable facts that the area to be examined harbors an individual posing a danger to those in the area of the apprehension.

(h) *Searches within Jails, Confinement Facilities, or Similar Facilities.* Evidence obtained from a search within a jail, confinement facility, or similar facility is admissible even if conducted without probable cause provided that it was authorized by persons with authority over the institution.

(i) *Emergency Searches to Save Life or for Related Purposes.* Evidence obtained from emergency searches of persons or property conducted to save life, or for a related purpose, is admissible provided that the search was conducted in a good faith effort to render immediate medical aid, to obtain information that will assist in the rendering of such aid, or to prevent immediate or ongoing personal injury.

(j) *Searches of Open Fields or Woodlands.* Evidence obtained from a search of an open field or woodland is admissible provided that the search was not unlawful within the meaning of Mil. R. Evid. 311.

Rule 315. Probable Cause Searches

(a) *General Rule.* Evidence obtained from reasonable searches conducted pursuant to a search warrant or search authorization, or under the exigent circumstances described in this rule, is admissible at trial when relevant and not otherwise inadmissible under these rules or the Constitution of the United States as applied to members of the armed forces.

(b) *Definitions.* As used in these rules:

(1) "Search authorization" means express permission, written or oral, issued by competent military authority to search a person or an area for specified property or evidence or for a specific person and to seize such property, evidence, or person. It may contain an order directing subordinate personnel to conduct a search in a specified manner.

(2) "Search warrant" means express permission to search and seize issued by competent civilian authority.

(c) *Scope of Search Authorization.* A search authorization may be valid under this rule for a search of:

(1) the physical person of anyone subject to military law or the law of war wherever found;

(2) military property of the United States or of nonappropriated fund activities of an armed force of the United States wherever located;

(3) persons or property situated on or in a military installation, encampment, vessel, aircraft, vehicle, or any other location under military control, wherever located; or

(4) nonmilitary property within a foreign country.

(d) *Who May Authorize.* A search authorization under this rule is valid only if issued by an impartial individual in one of the categories set forth in subdivisions (d)(1) and (d)(2). An otherwise impartial authorizing official does not

12

lose impartiality merely because he or she is present at the scene of a search or is otherwise readily available to persons who may seek the issuance of a search authorization; nor does such an official lose impartial character merely because the official previously and impartially authorized investigative activities when such previous authorization is similar in intent or function to a pretrial authorization made by the United States district courts.

(1) *Commander.* A commander or other person serving in a position designated by the Secretary concerned as either a position analogous to an officer in charge or a position of command, who has control over the place where the property or person to be searched is situated or found, or, if that place is not under military control, having control over persons subject to military law or the law of war; or

(2) *Military Judge or Magistrate.* A military judge or magistrate if authorized under regulations prescribed by the Secretary of Defense or the Secretary concerned.

(e) *Who May Search.*

(1) *Search Authorization.* Any commissioned officer, warrant officer, petty officer, noncommissioned officer, and, when in the execution of guard or police duties, any criminal investigator, member of the Air Force security forces, military police, or shore patrol, or person designated by proper authority to perform guard or police duties, or any agent of any such person, may conduct or authorize a search when a search authorization has been granted under this rule or a search would otherwise be proper under subdivision (g).

(2) *Search Warrants.* Any civilian or military criminal investigator authorized to request search warrants pursuant to applicable law or regulation is authorized to serve and execute search warrants. The execution of a search warrant affects admissibility only insofar as exclusion of evidence is required by the Constitution of the United States or an applicable federal statute.

(f) *Basis for Search Authorizations.*

(1) *Probable Cause Requirement.* A search authorization issued under this rule must be based upon probable cause.

(2) *Probable Cause Determination.* Probable cause to search exists when there is a reasonable belief that the person, property, or evidence sought is located in the place or on the person to be searched. A search authorization may be based upon hearsay evidence in whole or in part. A determination of probable cause under this rule will be based upon any or all of the following:

(A) written statements communicated to the authorizing official;

(B) oral statements communicated to the authorizing official in person, via telephone, or by other appropriate means of communication; or

(C) such information as may be known by the authorizing official that would not preclude the officer from acting in an impartial fashion. The Secretary of Defense or the Secretary concerned may prescribe additional requirements through regulation.

(g) *Exigencies.* Evidence obtained from a probable cause search is admissible without a search warrant or search authorization when there is a reasonable belief that the delay necessary to obtain a search warrant or search authorization would result in the removal, destruction, or concealment of the property or evidence sought. Military operational necessity may create an exigency by prohibiting or preventing communication with a person empowered to grant a search authorization.

Rule 316. Seizures

(a) *General Rule.* Evidence obtained from reasonable seizures is admissible at trial when relevant and not otherwise inadmissible under these rules or the Constitution of the United States as applied to members of the armed forces.

(b) *Apprehension.* Apprehension is governed by R.C.M. 302.

(c) *Seizure of Property or Evidence.*

(1) *Based on Probable Cause.* Evidence is admissible when seized based on a reasonable belief that the property or evidence is an unlawful weapon, contraband, evidence of crime, or might be used to resist apprehension or to escape.

(2) *Abandoned Property.* Abandoned property may be seized without probable cause and without a search warrant or search authorization. Such seizure may be made by any person.

(3) *Consent.* Property or evidence may be seized with consent consistent with the requirements applicable to consensual searches under Mil. R. Evid. 314.

(4) *Government Property.* Government property may be seized without probable cause and without a search warrant or search authorization by any person listed in subdivision (d), unless the person to whom the property is

13

issued or assigned has a reasonable expectation of privacy therein, as provided in Mil. R. Evid. 314(d), at the time of the seizure.

(5) *Other Property.* Property or evidence not included in subdivisions (c)(1)-(4) may be seized for use in evidence by any person listed in subdivision (d) if:

(A) *Authorization.* The person is authorized to seize the property or evidence by a search warrant or a search authorization under Mil. R. Evid. 315;

(B) *Exigent Circumstances.* The person has probable cause to seize the property or evidence and under Mil. R. Evid. 315(g) a search warrant or search authorization is not required; or

(C) *Plain View.* The person while in the course of otherwise lawful activity observes in a reasonable fashion property or evidence that the person has probable cause to seize.

(6) *Temporary Detention.* Nothing in this rule prohibits temporary detention of property on less than probable cause when authorized under the Constitution of the United States.

(d) *Who May Seize.* Any commissioned officer, warrant officer, petty officer, noncommissioned officer, and, when in the execution of guard or police duties, any criminal investigator, member of the Air Force security forces, military police, or shore patrol, or individual designated by proper authority to perform guard or police duties, or any agent of any such person, may seize property pursuant to this rule.

(e) *Other Seizures.* Evidence obtained from a seizure not addressed in this rule is admissible provided that its seizure was permissible under the Constitution of the United States as applied to members of the armed forces.

Rule 317. Interception of Wire and Oral Communications

(a) *General Rule.* Wire or oral communications constitute evidence obtained as a result of an unlawful search or seizure within the meaning of Mil. R. Evid. 311 when such evidence must be excluded under the Fourth Amendment to the Constitution of the United States as applied to members of the armed forces or if such evidence must be excluded under a federal statute applicable to members of the armed forces.

(b) *When Authorized by Court Order.* Evidence from the interception of wire or oral communications is admissible when authorized pursuant to an application to a federal judge of competent jurisdiction under the provisions of a federal statute.

(c) *Regulations.* Notwithstanding any other provision of these rules, evidence obtained by members of the armed forces or their agents through interception of wire or oral communications for law enforcement purposes is not admissible unless such interception:

(1) takes place in the United States and is authorized under subdivision (b);

(2) takes place outside the United States and is authorized under regulations issued by the Secretary of Defense or the Secretary concerned; or

(3) is authorized under regulations issued by the Secretary of Defense or the Secretary concerned and is not unlawful under applicable federal statutes.

Rule 321. Eyewitness Identification

(a) *General Rule.* Testimony concerning a relevant out-of-court identification by any person is admissible, subject to an appropriate objection under this rule, if such testimony is otherwise admissible under these rules. The witness making the identification and any person who has observed the previous identification may testify concerning it. When in testimony a witness identifies the accused as being, or not being, a participant in an offense or makes any other relevant identification concerning a person in the courtroom, evidence that on a previous occasion the witness made a similar identification is admissible to corroborate the witness's testimony as to identity even if the credibility of the witness has not been attacked directly, subject to appropriate objection under this rule.

(b) *When Inadmissible.* An identification of the accused as being a participant in an offense, whether such identification is made at the trial or otherwise, is inadmissible against the accused if:

(1) The identification is the result of an unlawful lineup or other unlawful identification process, as defined in subdivision (c), conducted by the United States or other domestic authorities and the accused makes a timely motion to suppress or an objection to the evidence under this rule; or

(2) Exclusion of the evidence is required by the Due Process Clause of the Fifth Amendment to the Constitution of the United States as applied to members of the armed forces. Evidence other than an identification of the accused that is obtained as a result of the unlawful lineup or unlawful identification process is inadmissible against the accused if the accused makes a timely motion to suppress or an objection to the evidence under this rule and if

14

exclusion of the evidence is required under the Constitution of the United States as applied to members of the armed forces.

(c) *Unlawful Lineup or Identification Process.*

(1) *Unreliable.* A lineup or other identification process is unreliable, and therefore unlawful, if the lineup or other identification process is so suggestive as to create a substantial likelihood of misidentification.

(2) *In Violation of Right to Counsel.* A lineup is unlawful if it is conducted in violation of the accused's rights to counsel.

(A) *Military Lineups.* An accused or suspect is entitled to counsel if, after preferral of charges or imposition of pretrial restraint under R.C.M. 304 for the offense under investigation, the accused is required by persons subject to the code or their agents to participate in a lineup for the purpose of identification. When a person entitled to counsel under this rule requests counsel, a judge advocate or a person certified in accordance with Article 27(b) will be provided by the United States at no expense to the accused or suspect and without regard to indigency or lack thereof before the lineup may proceed. The accused or suspect may waive the rights provided in this rule if the waiver is freely, knowingly, and intelligently made.

(B) *Nonmilitary Lineups.* When a person subject to the code is required to participate in a lineup for purposes of identification by an official or agent of the United States, of the District of Columbia, or of a State, Commonwealth, or possession of the United States, or any political subdivision of such a State, Commonwealth, or possession, and the provisions of subdivision (c)(2)(A) do not apply, the person's entitlement to counsel and the validity of any waiver of applicable rights will be determined by the principles of law generally recognized in the trial of criminal cases in the United States district courts involving similar lineups.

(d) *Motions to Suppress and Objections.*

(1) *Disclosure.* Prior to arraignment, the prosecution must disclose to the defense all evidence of, or derived from, a prior identification of the accused as a lineup or other identification process that it intends to offer into evidence against the accused at trial.

(2) *Time Requirement.* When such evidence has been disclosed, any motion to suppress or objection under this rule must be made by the defense prior to submission of a plea. In the absence of such motion or objection, the defense may not raise the issue at a later time except as permitted by the military judge for good cause shown. Failure to so move constitutes a waiver of the motion or objection.

(3) *Continuing Duty.* If the prosecution intends to offer such evidence and the evidence was not disclosed prior to arraignment, the prosecution must provide timely notice to the military judge and counsel for the accused. The defense may enter an objection at that time and the military judge may make such orders as are required in the interests of justice.

(4) *Specificity.* The military judge may require the defense to specify the grounds upon which the defense moves to suppress or object to evidence. If defense counsel, despite the exercise of due diligence, has been unable to interview adequately those persons involved in the lineup or other identification process, the military judge may enter any order required by the interests of justice, including authorization for the defense to make a general motion to suppress or a general objection.

(5) *Defense Evidence.* The defense may present evidence relevant to the issue of the admissibility of evidence as to which there has been an appropriate motion or objection under this rule. An accused may testify for the limited purpose of contesting the legality of the lineup or identification process giving rise to the challenged evidence. Prior to the introduction of such testimony by the accused, the defense must inform the military judge that the testimony is offered under subdivision (d). When the accused testifies under subdivision (d), the accused may be cross-examined only as to the matter on which he or she testifies. Nothing said by the accused on either direct or cross-examination may be used against the accused for any purpose other than in a prosecution for perjury, false swearing, or the making of a false official statement.

(6) *Burden and Standard of Proof.* When the defense has raised a specific motion or objection under subdivision (d)(3), the burden on the prosecution extends only to the grounds upon which the defense moved to suppress or object to the evidence.

(A) *Right to Counsel.*

(i) *Initial Violation of Right to Counsel at a Lineup.* When the accused raises the right to presence of counsel under this rule, the prosecution must prove by a preponderance of the evidence that counsel was present at the lineup or that the accused, having been advised of the right to the presence of counsel, voluntarily and intelligently waived that right prior to the lineup.

(ii) *Identification Subsequent to a Lineup Conducted in Violation of the Right to Counsel.* When the military judge determines that an identification is the result of a lineup conducted without the presence of counsel or

15

an appropriate waiver, any later identification by one present at such unlawful lineup is also a result thereof unless the military judge determines that the contrary has been shown by clear and convincing evidence.

     (B) *Unreliable Identification.*

          (i) *Initial Unreliable Identification.* When an objection raises the issue of an unreliable identification, the prosecution must prove by a preponderance of the evidence that the identification was reliable under the circumstances.

          (ii) *Identification Subsequent to an Unreliable Identification.* When the military judge determines that an identification is the result of an unreliable identification, a later identification may be admitted if the prosecution proves by clear and convincing evidence that the later identification is not the result of the inadmissible identification.

     (7) *Rulings.* A motion to suppress or an objection to evidence made prior to plea under this rule will be ruled upon prior to plea unless the military judge, for good cause, orders that it be deferred for determination at the trial of the general issue or until after findings, but no such determination will be deferred if a party's right to appeal the ruling is affected adversely. Where factual issues are involved in ruling upon such motion or objection, the military judge will state his or her essential findings of fact on the record.

(e) *Effect of Guilty Pleas.* Except as otherwise expressly provided in R.C.M. 910(a)(2), a plea of guilty to an offense that results in a finding of guilty waives all issues under this rule with respect to that offense whether or not raised prior to the plea.

Rule 401. Test for Relevant Evidence

Evidence is relevant if:

(a) it has any tendency to make a fact more or less probable than it would be without the evidence; and

(b) the fact is of consequence in determining the action.

Rule 402. General Admissibility of Relevant Evidence

(a) Relevant evidence is admissible unless any of the following provides otherwise:

     (1) the United States Constitution as it applies to members of the armed forces ;

     (2) a federal statute applicable to trial by courts-martial;

     (3) these rules; or

     (4) this Manual.

(b) Irrelevant evidence is not admissible.

Rule 403. Excluding Relevant Evidence for Prejudice, Confusion, Waste of Time, or Other Reasons

The military judge may exclude relevant evidence if its probative value is substantially outweighed by a danger of one or more of the following: unfair prejudice, confusing the issues, misleading the members, undue delay, wasting time, or needlessly presenting cumulative evidence.

Rule 404. Character Evidence; Crimes or Other Acts

(a) *Character Evidence.*

     (1) *Prohibited Uses.* Evidence of a person's character or character trait is not admissible to prove that on a particular occasion the person acted in accordance with the character or trait.

     (2) *Exceptions for an Accused or Victim.*

          (A) The accused may offer evidence of the accused's pertinent trait, and if the evidence is admitted, the prosecution may offer evidence to rebut it.

          (B) Subject to the limitations in Mil. R. Evid. 412, the accused may offer evidence of an alleged victim's pertinent trait, and if the evidence is admitted, the prosecution may:

               (i) offer evidence to rebut it; and

               (ii) offer evidence of the accused's same trait; and

          (C) in a homicide or assault case, the prosecution may offer evidence of the alleged victim's trait of peacefulness to rebut evidence that the victim was the first aggressor.

     (3) *Exceptions for a Witness.* Evidence of a witness's character may be admitted under Mil R. Evid. 607, 608, and 609.

16

(b) *Crimes, Wrongs, or Other Acts.*

(1) *Prohibited Uses.* Evidence of a crime, wrong, or other act is not admissible to prove a person's character in order to show that on a particular occasion the person acted in accordance with the character.

(2) *Permitted Uses; Notice.* This evidence may be admissible for another purpose, such as proving motive, opportunity, intent, preparation, plan, knowledge, identity, absence of mistake, or lack of accident. On request by the accused, the prosecution must:

(A) provide reasonable notice of the general nature of any such evidence that the prosecution intends to offer at trial; and

(B) do so before trial – or during trial if the military judge, for good cause, excuses lack of pretrial notice.

Rule 405. Methods of Proving Character

(a) *By Reputation or Opinion.* When evidence of a person's character or character trait is admissible, it may be proved by testimony about the person's reputation or by testimony in the form of an opinion. On cross-examination of the character witness, the military judge may allow an inquiry into relevant specific instances of the person's conduct.

(b) *By Specific Instances of Conduct.* When a person's character or character trait is an essential element of a charge, claim, or defense, the character or trait may also be proved by relevant specific instances of the person's conduct.

(c) *By Affidavit.* The defense may introduce affidavits or other written statements of persons other than the accused concerning the character of the accused. If the defense introduces affidavits or other written statements under this subdivision, the prosecution may, in rebuttal, also introduce affidavits or other written statements regarding the character of the accused. Evidence of this type may be introduced by the defense or prosecution only if, aside from being contained in an affidavit or other written statement, it would otherwise be admissible under these rules.

(d) *Definitions.* "Reputation" means the estimation in which a person generally is held in the community in which the person lives or pursues a business or profession. "Community" in the armed forces includes a post, camp, ship, station, or other military organization regardless of size.

Rule 406. Habit; Routine Practice

Evidence of a person's habit or an organization's routine practice may be admitted to prove that on a particular occasion the person or organization acted in accordance with the habit or routine practice. The military judge may admit this evidence regardless of whether it is corroborated or whether there was an eyewitness.

Rule 407. Subsequent Remedial Measures

(a) When measures are taken that would have made an earlier injury or harm less likely to occur, evidence of the subsequent measures is not admissible to prove:

(1) negligence;

(2) culpable conduct;

(3) a defect in a product or its design; or

(4) a need for a warning or instruction.

(b) The military judge may admit this evidence for another purpose, such as impeachment or – if disputed – proving ownership, control, or the feasibility of precautionary measures.

Rule 408. Compromise Offers and Negotiations

(a) *Prohibited Uses.* Evidence of the following is not admissible – on behalf of any party – either to prove or disprove the validity or amount of a disputed claim or to impeach by a prior inconsistent statement or a contradiction:

(1) furnishing, promising, or offering – or accepting, promising to accept, or offering to accept – a valuable consideration in order to compromise the claim; and

(2) conduct or a statement made during compromise negotiations about the claim – except when the negotiations related to a claim by a public office in the exercise of its regulatory, investigative, or enforcement authority.

(b) *Exceptions.* The military judge may admit this evidence for another purpose, such as proving witness bias or prejudice, negating a contention of undue delay, or proving an effort to obstruct a criminal investigation or prosecution.

17

Rule 409. Offers to Pay Medical and Similar Expenses

Evidence of furnishing, promising to pay, or offering to pay medical, hospital, or similar expenses resulting from an injury is not admissible to prove liability for the injury.

Rule 410. Pleas, Plea Discussions, and Related Statements

(a) *Prohibited Uses.* Evidence of the following is not admissible against the accused who made the plea or participated in the plea discussions:

   (1) a guilty plea that was later withdrawn;

   (2) a nolo contendere plea;

   (3) any statement made in the course of any judicial inquiry regarding either of the foregoing pleas; or

   (4) any statement made during plea discussions with the convening authority, staff judge advocate, trial counsel or other counsel for the government if the discussions did not result in a guilty plea or they resulted in a later-withdrawn guilty plea.

(b) *Exceptions.* The military judge may admit a statement described in subdivision (a)(3) or (a)(4):

   (1) when another statement made during the same plea or plea discussions has been introduced, if in fairness the statements ought to be considered together; or

   (2) in a proceeding for perjury or false statement, if the accused made the statement under oath, on the record, and with counsel present.

(c) *Request for Administrative Disposition.* A "statement made during plea discussions" includes a statement made by the accused solely for the purpose of requesting disposition under an authorized procedure for administrative action in lieu of trial by court-martial; "on the record" includes the written statement submitted by the accused in furtherance of such request.

Rule 411. Liability Insurance

Evidence that a person was or was not insured against liability is not admissible to prove whether the person acted negligently or otherwise wrongfully. The military judge may admit this evidence for another purpose, such as proving witness bias or prejudice or proving agency, ownership, or control.

Rule 412. Sex Offense Cases: The Victim's Sexual Behavior or Predisposition

[No change to current version of M.R.E. 412]

Rule 413. Similar Crimes in Sexual Offense Cases

(a) *Permitted Uses.* In a court-martial proceeding for a sexual offense, the military judge may admit evidence that the accused committed any other sexual offense. The evidence may be considered on any matter to which it is relevant.

(b) *Disclosure to the Accused.* If the prosecution intends to offer this evidence, the prosecution must disclose it to the accused, including any witnesses' statements or a summary of the expected testimony. The prosecution must do so at least 5 days prior to entry of pleas or at a later time that the military judge allows for good cause.

(c) *Effect on Other Rules.* This rule does not limit the admission or consideration of evidence under any other rule.

(d) *Definition.* As used in this rule, "sexual offense" means an offense punishable under the Uniform Code of Military Justice, or a crime under federal or state law (as "state" is defined in 18 U.S.C. § 513), involving:

   (1) any conduct prohibited by Article 120;

   (2) any conduct prohibited by 18 U.S.C. chapter 109A;

   (3) contact, without consent, between any part of the accused's body, or an object held or controlled by the accused, and another person's genitals or anus;

   (4) contact, without consent, between the accused's genitals or anus and any part of another person's body;

   (5) contact with the aim of deriving sexual pleasure or gratification from inflicting death, bodily injury, or physical pain on another person; or

   (6) an attempt or conspiracy to engage in conduct described in subdivisions (d)(1)-(5).

18

Rule 414. Similar Crimes in Child-Molestation Cases

(a) *Permitted Uses*. In a court-martial proceeding in which an accused is charged with an act of child molestation, the military judge may admit evidence that the accused committed any other offense of child molestation. The evidence may be considered on any matter to which it is relevant.

(b) *Disclosure to the Accused*. If the prosecution intends to offer this evidence, the prosecution must disclose it to the accused, including witnesses' statements or a summary of the expected testimony. The prosecution must do so at least 5 days prior to entry of pleas or at a later time that the military judge allows for good cause.

(c) *Effect on Other Rules*. This rule does not limit the admission or consideration of evidence under any other rule.

(d) *Definitions*. As used in this rule:

    (1) "Child" means a person below the age of 16; and

    (2) "Child molestation" means an offense punishable under the Uniform Code of Military Justice, or a crime under federal law or under state law (as "state" is defined in 18 U.S.C. § 513), that involves:

        (A) any conduct prohibited by Article 120 and committed with a child;

        (B) any conduct prohibited by 18 U.S.C. chapter 109A and committed with a child;

        (C) any conduct prohibited by 18 U.S.C. chapter 110;

        (D) contact between any part of the accused's body, or an object held or controlled by the accused, and a child's genitals or anus;

        (E) contact between the accused's genitals or anus and any part of a child's body;

        (F) contact with the aim of deriving sexual pleasure or gratification from inflicting death, bodily injury, or physical pain on a child; or

        (G) an attempt or conspiracy to engage in conduct described in subdivisions (d)(2)(A)-(F).

Rule 501. Privilege in General

(a) A person may not claim a privilege with respect to any matter except as required by or provided for in:

    (1) the United States Constitution as applied to members of the armed forces;

    (2) a federal statute applicable to trials by courts-martial;

    (3) these rules;

    (4) this Manual; or

    (4) the principles of common law generally recognized in the trial of criminal cases in the United States district courts under rule 501 of the Federal Rules of Evidence, insofar as the application of such principles in trials by courts-martial is practicable and not contrary to or inconsistent with the Uniform Code of Military Justice, these rules, or this Manual.

(b) A claim of privilege includes, but is not limited to, the assertion by any person of a privilege to:

    (1) refuse to be a witness;

    (2) refuse to disclose any matter;

    (3) refuse to produce any object or writing; or

    (4) prevent another from being a witness or disclosing any matter or producing any object or writing.

(c) The term "person" includes an appropriate representative of the Federal Government, a State, or political subdivision thereof, or any other entity claiming to be the holder of a privilege.

(d) Notwithstanding any other provision of these rules, information not otherwise privileged does not become privileged on the basis that it was acquired by a medical officer or civilian physician in a professional capacity.

Rule 502. Lawyer-Client Privilege

(a) *General Rule*. A client has a privilege to refuse to disclose and to prevent any other person from disclosing confidential communications made for the purpose of facilitating the rendition of professional legal services to the client:

    (1) between the client or the client's representative and the lawyer or the lawyer's representative;

    (2) between the lawyer and the lawyer's representative;

    (3) by the client or the client's lawyer to a lawyer representing another in a matter of common interest;

    (4) between representatives of the client or between the client and a representative of the client; or

    (5) between lawyers representing the client.

(b) *Definitions*. As used in this rule:

19

(1) "Client" means a person, public officer, corporation, association, organization, or other entity, either public or private, who receives professional legal services from a lawyer, or who consults a lawyer with a view to obtaining professional legal services from the lawyer.

(2) "Lawyer" means a person authorized, or reasonably believed by the client to be authorized, to practice law; or a member of the armed forces detailed, assigned, or otherwise provided to represent a person in a court-martial case or in any military investigation or proceeding. The term "lawyer" does not include a member of the armed forces serving in a capacity other than as a judge advocate, legal officer, or law specialist as defined in Article 1, unless the member:

(A) is detailed, assigned, or otherwise provided to represent a person in a court-martial case or in any military investigation or proceeding;

(B) is authorized by the armed forces, or reasonably believed by the client to be authorized, to render professional legal services to members of the armed forces; or

(C) is authorized to practice law and renders professional legal services during off-duty employment.

(3) "Lawyer's representative" means a person employed by or assigned to assist a lawyer in providing professional legal services.

(4) A communication is "confidential" if not intended to be disclosed to third persons other than those to whom disclosure is in furtherance of the rendition of professional legal services to the client or those reasonably necessary for the transmission of the communication.

(c) *Who May Claim the Privilege.* The privilege may be claimed by the client, the guardian or conservator of the client, the personal representative of a deceased client, or the successor, trustee, or similar representative of a corporation, association, or other organization, whether or not in existence. The lawyer or the lawyer's representative who received the communication may claim the privilege on behalf of the client. The authority of the lawyer to do so is presumed in the absence of evidence to the contrary.

(d) *Exceptions.* There is no privilege under this rule under any of the following circumstances:

(1) *Crime or Fraud.* If the communication clearly contemplated the future commission of a fraud or crime or if services of the lawyer were sought or obtained to enable or aid anyone to commit or plan to commit what the client knew or reasonably should have known to be a crime or fraud;

(2) *Claimants through Same Deceased Client.* As to a communication relevant to an issue between parties who claim through the same deceased client, regardless of whether the claims are by testate or intestate succession or by inter vivos transaction;

(3) *Breach of Duty by Lawyer or Client.* As to a communication relevant to an issue of breach of duty by the lawyer to the client or by the client to the lawyer;

(4) *Document Attested by the Lawyer.* As to a communication relevant to an issue concerning an attested document to which the lawyer is an attesting witness; or

(5) *Joint Clients.* As to a communication relevant to a matter of common interest between two or more clients if the communication was made by any of them to a lawyer retained or consulted in common, when offered in an action between any of the clients.

Rule 503. Communications to Clergy

(a) *General Rule.* A person has a privilege to refuse to disclose and to prevent another from disclosing a confidential communication by the person to a clergyman or to a clergyman's assistant, if such communication is made either as a formal act of religion or as a matter of conscience.

(b) *Definitions.* As used in this rule:

(1) "Clergyman" means a minister, priest, rabbi, chaplain, or other similar functionary of a religious organization, or an individual reasonably believed to be so by the person consulting the clergyman.

(2) "Clergyman's assistant" means a person employed by or assigned to assist a clergyman in his capacity as a spiritual advisor.

(3) A communication is "confidential" if made to a clergyman in the clergyman's capacity as a spiritual adviser or to a clergyman's assistant in the assistant's official capacity and is not intended to be disclosed to third persons other than those to whom disclosure is in furtherance of the purpose of the communication or to those reasonably necessary for the transmission of the communication."

(c) *Who May Claim the Privilege.* The privilege may be claimed by the person, guardian, or conservator, or by a personal representative if the person is deceased. The clergyman or clergyman's assistant who received the

20

communication may claim the privilege on behalf of the person. The authority of the clergyman or clergyman's assistant to do so is presumed in the absence of evidence to the contrary.

Rule 504. Husband-Wife Privilege

(a) *Spousal Incapacity.* A person has a privilege to refuse to testify against his or her spouse.

(b) *Confidential Communication Made During the Marriage.*

(1) *General Rule.* A person has a privilege during and after the marital relationship to refuse to disclose, and to prevent another from disclosing, any confidential communication made to the spouse of the person while they were husband and wife and not separated as provided by law.

(2) *Definition.* As used in this rule, a communication is "confidential" if made privately by any person to the spouse of the person and is not intended to be disclosed to third persons other than those reasonably necessary for transmission of the communication.

(3) *Who May Claim the Privilege.* The privilege may be claimed by the spouse who made the communication or by the other spouse on his or her behalf. The authority of the latter spouse to do so is presumed in the absence of evidence of a waiver. The privilege will not prevent disclosure of the communication at the request of the spouse to whom the communication was made if that spouse is an accused regardless of whether the spouse who made the communication objects to its disclosure.

(c) *Exceptions.*

(1) *To Spousal Incapacity Only.* There is no privilege under subdivision (a) when, at the time the testimony of one of the parties to the marriage is to be introduced in evidence against the other party, the parties are divorced or the marriage has been annulled.

(2) *To Spousal Incapacity and Confidential Communications.* There is no privilege under subdivisions (a) or (b):

(A) In proceedings in which one spouse is charged with a crime against the person or property of the other spouse or a child of either, or with a crime against the person or property of a third person committed in the course of committing a crime against the other spouse;

(B) When the marital relationship was entered into with no intention of the parties to live together as spouses, but only for the purpose of using the purported marital relationship as a sham, and with respect to the privilege in subdivision (a), the relationship remains a sham at the time the testimony or statement of one of the parties is to be introduced against the other; or with respect to the privilege in subdivision (b), the relationship was a sham at the time of the communication; or

(C) In proceedings in which a spouse is charged, in accordance with Article 133 or 134, with importing the other spouse as an alien for prostitution or other immoral purpose in violation of 18 U.S.C. §1328; with transporting the other spouse in interstate commerce for immoral purposes or other offense in violation of 18 U.S.C. §§ 2421–2424; or with violation of such other similar statutes under which such privilege may not be claimed in the trial of criminal cases in the United States district courts.

(D) Where both parties have been substantial participants in illegal activity, those communications between the spouses during the marriage regarding the illegal activity in which they have jointly participated are not marital communications for purposes of the privilege in subdivision (b) and are not entitled to protection under the privilege in subdivision (b).

(d) *Definitions.* As used in this rule:

(1) "A child of either" means a biological child, adopted child, or ward of one of the spouses and includes a child who is under the permanent or temporary physical custody of one of the spouses, regardless of the existence of a legal parent-child relationship. For purposes of this rule only, a child is:

(A) an individual under the age of 18; or

(B) an individual with a mental handicap who functions under the age of 18.

(2) "Temporary physical custody" means a parent has entrusted his or her child with another. There is no minimum amount of time necessary to establish temporary physical custody, nor is a written agreement required. Rather, the focus is on the parent's agreement with another for assuming parental responsibility for the child. For example, temporary physical custody may include instances where a parent entrusts another with the care of their child for recurring care or during absences due to temporary duty or deployments.

21

Rule 505. Classified Information

(a) *General Rule.* Classified information must be protected and is privileged from disclosure if disclosure would be detrimental to the national security. Under no circumstances may a military judge order the release of classified information to any person not authorized to receive such information. The Secretary of Defense may prescribe security procedures for protection against the compromise of classified information submitted to courts-martial and appellate authorities.

(b) *Definitions.* As used in this rule:

(1) "Classified information" means any information or material that has been determined by the United States Government pursuant to an executive order, statute, or regulations, to require protection against unauthorized disclosure for reasons of national security, and any restricted data, as defined in 42 U.S.C. § 2014(y).

(2) "National security" means the national defense and foreign relations of the United States.

(3) "In camera hearing" means a session under Article 39(a) from which the public is excluded.

(4) "In camera review" means an inspection of documents or other evidence conducted by the military judge alone in chambers and not on the record.

(5) "Ex parte" means a discussion between the military judge and either the defense counsel or prosecution, without the other party or the public present. This discussion can be on or off the record, depending on the circumstances. The military judge will grant a request for an ex parte discussion or hearing only after finding that such discussion or hearing is necessary to protect classified information or other good cause. Prior to granting a request from one party for an ex parte discussion or hearing, the military judge must provide notice to the opposing party on the record. If the ex parte discussion is conducted off the record, the military judge should later state on the record that such ex parte discussion took place and generally summarize the subject matter of the discussion, as appropriate.

(c) *Access to Evidence.* Any information admitted into evidence pursuant to any rule, procedure, or order by the military judge must be provided to the accused.

(d) *Declassification.* Trial counsel should, when practicable, seek declassification of evidence that may be used at trial, consistent with the requirements of national security. A decision not to declassify evidence under this section is not subject to review by a military judge or upon appeal.

(e) *Action Prior to Referral of Charges.*

(1) Prior to referral of charges, upon a showing by the accused that the classified information sought is relevant and necessary to an element of the offense or a legally cognizable defense, the convening authority must respond in writing to a request by the accused for classified information if the privilege in this rule is claimed for such information. In response to such a request, the convening authority may:

(A) delete specified items of classified information from documents made available to the accused;

(B) substitute a portion or summary of the information for such classified documents;

(C) substitute a statement admitting relevant facts that the classified information would tend to prove;

(D) provide the document subject to conditions that will guard against the compromise of the information disclosed to the accused; or

(E) withhold disclosure if actions under (A) through (D) cannot be taken without causing identifiable damage to the national security.

(2) An Article 32 investigating officer may not rule on any objection by the accused to the release of documents or information protected by this rule.

(3) Any objection by the accused to the withholding of information or to the conditions of disclosure must be raised through a motion for appropriate relief at a pretrial conference.

(f) *Actions after Referral of Charges.*

(1) *Pretrial Conference.* At any time after referral of charges, any party may move for a pretrial conference under Article 39(a) to consider matters relating to classified information that may arise in connection with the trial. Following such a motion, or when the military judge recognizes the need for such conference, the military judge must promptly hold a pretrial conference under Article 39(a).

(2) *Ex Parte Permissible.* Upon request by either party and with a showing of good cause, the military judge must hold such conference ex parte to the extent necessary to protect classified information from disclosure.

(3) *Matters to be Established at Pretrial Conference.*

(A) *Timing of Subsequent Actions.* At the pretrial conference, the military judge must establish the timing of:

22

(i) requests for discovery;

(ii) the provision of notice required by subdivision (i) of this rule; and

(iii) the initiation of the procedure established by subdivision (j) of this rule.

(B) *Other Matters.* At the pretrial conference, the military judge may also consider any matter that relates to classified information or that may promote a fair and expeditious trial.

(4) *Convening Authority Notice and Action.* If a claim of privilege has been made under this rule with respect to classified information that apparently contains evidence that is relevant and necessary to an element of the offense or a legally cognizable defense and is otherwise admissible in evidence in the court-martial proceeding, the matter must be reported to the convening authority. The convening authority may:

(A) institute action to obtain the classified information for the use by the military judge in making a determination under subdivision (j);

(B) dismiss the charges;

(C) dismiss the charges or specifications or both to which the information relates; or

(D) take such other action as may be required in the interests of justice.

(5) *Remedies.* If, after a reasonable period of time, the information is not provided to the military judge in circumstances where proceeding with the case without such information would materially prejudice a substantial right of the accused, the military judge must dismiss the charges or specifications or both to which the classified information relates.

(g) *Protective Orders.* Upon motion of the trial counsel, the military judge must issue an order to protect against the disclosure of any classified information that has been disclosed by the United States to any accused in any court-martial proceeding or that has otherwise been provided to, or obtained by, any such accused in any such court-martial proceeding. The terms of any such protective order may include, but are not limited to, provisions:

(1) prohibiting the disclosure of the information except as authorized by the military judge;

(2) requiring storage of material in a manner appropriate for the level of classification assigned to the documents to be disclosed;

(3) requiring controlled access to the material during normal business hours and at other times upon reasonable notice;

(4) mandating that all persons requiring security clearances will cooperate with investigatory personnel in any investigations that are necessary to obtain a security clearance;

(5) requiring the maintenance of logs regarding access by all persons authorized by the military judge to have access to the classified information in connection with the preparation of the defense;

(6) regulating the making and handling of notes taken from material containing classified information; or

(7) requesting the convening authority to authorize the assignment of government security personnel and the provision of government storage facilities.

(h) *Discovery and Access by the Accused.*

(1) *Limitations.*

(A) *Government Claim of Privilege.* In a court-martial proceeding in which the government seeks to delete, withhold, or otherwise obtain other relief with respect to the discovery of or access to any classified information, the trial counsel must submit a declaration invoking the United States' classified information privilege and setting forth the damage to the national security that the discovery of or access to such information reasonably could be expected to cause. The declaration must be signed by the head, or designee, of the executive or military department or government agency concerned.

(B) *Standard for Discovery or Access by the Accused.* Upon the submission of a declaration under subdivision (h)(1)(A), the military judge may not authorize the discovery of or access to such classified information unless the military judge determines that such classified information would be noncumulative and relevant to a legally cognizable defense, rebuttal of the prosecution's case, or to sentencing. If the discovery of or access to such classified information is authorized, it must be addressed in accordance with the requirements of subdivision (h)(2).

(2) *Alternatives to Full Discovery.*

(A) *Substitutions and Other Alternatives.* The military judge, in assessing the accused's right to discover or access classified information under subdivision (h), may authorize the government:

(i) to delete or withhold specified items of classified information;

(ii) to substitute a summary for classified information; or

(iii) to substitute a statement admitting relevant facts that the classified information or material would tend to prove, unless the military judge determines that disclosure of the classified information itself is necessary to enable the accused to prepare for trial.

(B) *In Camera Review*. The military judge must, upon the request of the prosecution, conduct an in camera review of the prosecution's motion and any materials submitted in support thereof and must not disclose such information to the accused.

(C) *Action by Military Judge*. The military judge must grant the request of the trial counsel to substitute a summary or to substitute a statement admitting relevant facts, or to provide other relief in accordance with subdivision (h)(2)(A), if the military judge finds that the summary, statement, or other relief would provide the accused with substantially the same ability to make a defense as would discovery of or access to the specific classified information.

(3) *Reconsideration*. An order of a military judge authorizing a request of the trial counsel to substitute, summarize, withhold, or prevent access to classified information under subdivision (h) is not subject to a motion for reconsideration by the accused, if such order was entered pursuant to an ex parte showing under subdivision (h).

(i) *Disclosure by the Accused.*

(1) *Notification to Trial Counsel and Military Judge*. If an accused reasonably expects to disclose, or to cause the disclosure of, classified information in any manner in connection with any trial or pretrial proceeding involving the prosecution of such accused, the accused must, within the time specified by the military judge or, where no time is specified, prior to arraignment of the accused, notify the trial counsel and the military judge in writing.

(2) *Content of Notice*. Such notice must include a brief description of the classified information.

(3) *Continuing Duty to Notify*. Whenever the accused learns of additional classified information the accused reasonably expects to disclose, or to cause the disclosure of, at any such proceeding, the accused must notify trial counsel and the military judge in writing as soon as possible thereafter and must include a brief description of the classified information.

(4) *Limitation on Disclosure by Accused*. The accused may not disclose, or cause the disclosure of, any information known or believed to be classified in connection with a trial or pretrial proceeding until:

(A) notice has been given under subdivision (i); and

(B) the government has been afforded a reasonable opportunity to seek a determination pursuant to the procedure set forth in subdivision (j).

(5) *Failure to comply*. If the accused fails to comply with the requirements of subdivision (i), the military judge:

(A) may preclude disclosure of any classified information not made the subject of notification; and

(B) may prohibit the examination by the accused of any witness with respect to any such information.

(j) *Procedure for Use of Classified Information in Trials and Pretrial Proceedings.*

(1) *Hearing on Use of Classified Information.*

(A) *Motion for Hearing*. Within the time specified by the military judge for the filing of a motion under this rule, either party may move for a hearing concerning the use at any proceeding of any classified information. Upon a request by either party, the military judge must conduct such a hearing and must rule prior to conducting any further proceedings.

(B) *Request for In Camera Hearing*. Any hearing held pursuant to subdivision (j) (or any portion of such hearing specified in the request of a knowledgeable United States official) must be held in camera if a knowledgeable United States official possessing authority to classify information submits to the military judge a declaration that a public proceeding may result in the disclosure of classified information.

(C) *Notice to Accused*. Before the hearing, trial counsel must provide the accused with notice of the classified information that is at issue. Such notice must identify the specific classified information at issue whenever that information previously has been made available to the accused by the United States. When the United States has not previously made the information available to the accused in connection with the case the information may be described by generic category, in such forms as the military judge may approve, rather than by identification of the specific information of concern to the United States.

(D) *Standard for Disclosure*. Classified information is not subject to disclosure under subdivision (j) unless the information is relevant and necessary to an element of the offense or a legally cognizable defense and is otherwise admissible in evidence. In presentencing proceedings, relevant and material classified information pertaining to the appropriateness of, or the appropriate degree of, punishment must be admitted only if no unclassified version of such information is available.

24

(E) *Written Findings.* As to each item of classified information, the military judge must set forth in writing the basis for the determination.

(2) *Alternatives to Full Disclosure.*

(A) *Motion by the Prosecution.* Upon any determination by the military judge authorizing the disclosure of specific classified information under the procedures established by subdivision (j), the trial counsel may move that, in lieu of the disclosure of such specific classified information, the military judge order:

(i)   the substitution for such classified information of a statement admitting relevant facts that the specific classified information would tend to prove;

(ii)   the substitution for such classified information of a summary of the specific classified information; or

(iii) any other procedure or redaction limiting the disclosure of specific classified information.

(B) *Declaration of Damage to National Security.* The trial counsel may, in connection with a motion under subdivision (j), submit to the military judge a declaration signed by the head, or designee, of the executive or military department or government agency concerned certifying that disclosure of classified information would cause identifiable damage to the national security of the United States and explaining the basis for the classification of such information. If so requested by the trial counsel, the military judge must examine such declaration during an in camera review.

(C) *Hearing.* The military judge must hold a hearing on any motion under subdivision (j). Any such hearing must be held in camera at the request of a knowledgeable United States official possessing authority to classify information.

(D) *Standard for Use of Alternatives.* The military judge must grant such a motion of the trial counsel if the military judge finds that the statement, summary, or other procedure or redaction will provide the accused with substantially the same ability to make his or her defense as would disclosure of the specific classified information.

(3) *Sealing of Records of In Camera Hearings.* If at the close of an in camera hearing under subdivision (j) (or any portion of a hearing under subdivision (j) that is held in camera), the military judge determines that the classified information at issue may not be disclosed or elicited at the trial or pretrial proceeding, the record of such in camera hearing must be sealed in accordance with R.C.M. 1103A and preserved for use in the event of an appeal. The accused may seek reconsideration of the military judge's determination prior to or during trial.

(4) *Remedies.*

(A) If the military judge determines that alternatives to full disclosure may not be used and the prosecution continues to object to disclosure of the information, the military judge must issue any order that the interests of justice require, including but not limited to, an order:

(i)   striking or precluding all or part of the testimony of a witness;

(ii)   declaring a mistrial;

(iii) finding against the government on any issue as to which the evidence is relevant and material to the defense;

(iv) dismissing the charges, with or without prejudice; or

(v)   dismissing the charges or specifications or both to which the information relates.

(B) The government may avoid the sanction for nondisclosure by permitting the accused to disclose the information at the pertinent court-martial proceeding.

(5) *Disclosure of Rebuttal Information.* Whenever the military judge determines that classified information may be disclosed in connection with a trial or pretrial proceeding, the military judge must, unless the interests of fairness do not so require, order the prosecution to provide the accused with the information it expects to use to rebut the classified information.

(A) *Continuing Duty.* The military judge may place the prosecution under a continuing duty to disclose such rebuttal information.

(B) *Sanction for Failure to Comply.* If the prosecution fails to comply with its obligation under subdivision (j), the military judge:

(i)   may exclude any evidence not made the subject of a required disclosure; and

(ii)   may prohibit the examination by the prosecution of any witness with respect to such information.

(6) *Disclosure at Trial of Previous Statements by a Witness.*

(A) *Motion for Production of Statements in Possession of the Prosecution.* After a witness called by the trial counsel has testified on direct examination, the military judge, on motion of the accused, may order production

25

of statements of the witness in the possession of the prosecution that relate to the subject matter as to which the witness has testified. This paragraph does not preclude discovery or assertion of a privilege otherwise authorized.

(B) *Invocation of Privilege by the Government.* If the government invokes a privilege, the trial counsel may provide the prior statements of the witness to the military judge for in camera review to the extent necessary to protect classified information from disclosure.

(C) *Action by Military Judge.* If the military judge finds that disclosure of any portion of the statement identified by the government as classified would be detrimental to the national security in the degree required to warrant classification under the applicable Executive Order, statute, or regulation, that such portion of the statement is consistent with the testimony of the witness, and that the disclosure of such portion is not necessary to afford the accused a fair trial, the military judge must excise that portion from the statement. If the military judge finds that such portion of the statement is inconsistent with the testimony of the witness or that its disclosure is necessary to afford the accused a fair trial, the military judge must, upon the request of the trial counsel, consider alternatives to disclosure in accordance with subdivision (j)(2).

(k) *Introduction into Evidence of Classified Information.*

(1) *Preservation of Classification Status.* Writings, recordings, and photographs containing classified information may be admitted into evidence in court-martial proceedings under this rule without change in their classification status.

(A) *Precautions.* The military judge in a trial by court-martial, in order to prevent unnecessary disclosure of classified information, may order admission into evidence of only part of a writing, recording, or photograph, or may order admission into evidence of the whole writing, recording, or photograph with excision of some or all of the classified information contained therein, unless the whole ought in fairness be considered.

(B) *Classified Information Kept Under Seal.* The military judge must allow classified information offered or accepted into evidence to remain under seal during the trial, even if such evidence is disclosed in the court-martial proceeding, and may, upon motion by the government, seal exhibits containing classified information in accordance with R.C.M. 1103A for any period after trial as necessary to prevent a disclosure of classified information when a knowledgeable United States official possessing authority to classify information submits to the military judge a declaration setting forth the damage to the national security that the disclosure of such information reasonably could be expected to cause.

(2) *Testimony.*

(A) *Objection by Trial Counsel.* During the examination of a witness, trial counsel may object to any question or line of inquiry that may require the witness to disclose classified information not previously found to be admissible.

(B) *Action by Military Judge.* Following an objection under subdivision (k), the military judge must take such suitable action to determine whether the response is admissible as will safeguard against the compromise of any classified information. Such action may include requiring trial counsel to provide the military judge with a proffer of the witness's response to the question or line of inquiry and requiring the accused to provide the military judge with a proffer of the nature of the information sought to be elicited by the accused. Upon request, the military judge may accept an ex parte proffer by trial counsel to the extent necessary to protect classified information from disclosure.

(3) *Closed session.* The military judge may, subject to the requirements of the United States Constitution, exclude the public during that portion of the presentation of evidence that discloses classified information.

(l) *Record of Trial.* If under this rule any information is withheld from the accused, the accused objects to such withholding, and the trial is continued to an adjudication of guilt of the accused, the entire unaltered text of the relevant documents as well as the prosecution's motion and any materials submitted in support thereof must be sealed in accordance with R.C.M. 1103A and attached to the record of trial as an appellate exhibit. Such material must be made available to reviewing authorities in closed proceedings for the purpose of reviewing the determination of the military judge. The record of trial with respect to any classified matter will be prepared under R.C.M. 1103(h) and 1104(b)(1)(D).

Rule 506. Government Information Other than Classified Information

(a) *Protection of Government Information.* Except where disclosure is required by a federal statute, government information is privileged from disclosure if disclosure would be detrimental to the public interest.

(b) *Scope.* "Government information" includes official communication and documents and other information within the custody or control of the Federal Government. This rule does not apply to classified information (Mil. R. Evid. 505) or to the identity of an informant (Mil. R. Evid. 507).

26

(c) *Definitions.* As used in this rule:

(1) "In camera hearing" means a session under Article 39(a) from which the public is excluded.

(2) "In camera review" means an inspection of documents or other evidence conducted by the military judge alone in chambers and not on the record.

(3) "Ex parte" means a discussion between the military judge and either the defense counsel or prosecution, without the other party or the public present. This discussion can be on or off the record, depending on the circumstances. The military judge will grant a request for an ex parte discussion or hearing only after finding that such discussion or hearing is necessary to protect government information or other good cause. Prior to granting a request from one party for an ex parte discussion or hearing, the military judge must provide notice to the opposing party on the record. If the ex parte discussion is conducted off the record, the military judge should later state on the record that such ex parte discussion took place and generally summarize the subject matter of the discussion, as appropriate.

(d) *Who May Claim the Privilege.* The privilege may be claimed by the head, or designee, of the executive or military department or government agency concerned. The privilege for records and information of the Inspector General may be claimed by the immediate superior of the inspector general officer responsible for creation of the records or information, the Inspector General, or any other superior authority. A person who may claim the privilege may authorize a witness or the trial counsel to claim the privilege on his or her behalf. The authority of a witness or the trial counsel to do so is presumed in the absence of evidence to the contrary.

(e) *Action Prior to Referral of Charges.*

(1) Prior to referral of charges, upon a showing by the accused that the government information sought is relevant and necessary to an element of the offense or a legally cognizable defense, the convening authority must respond in writing to a request by the accused for government information if the privilege in this rule is claimed for such information. In response to such a request, the convening authority may:

(A) delete specified items of government information claimed to be privileged from documents made available to the accused;

(B) substitute a portion or summary of the information for such documents;

(C) substitute a statement admitting relevant facts that the government information would tend to prove;

(D) provide the document subject to conditions similar to those set forth in subdivision (g) of this rule; or

(E) withhold disclosure if actions under subdivisions (e)(1)(1)-(4) cannot be taken without causing identifiable damage to the public interest.

(2) Any objection by the accused to withholding of information or to the conditions of disclosure must be raised through a motion for appropriate relief at a pretrial conference.

(f) *Action After Referral of Charges.*

(1) *Pretrial Conference.* At any time after referral of charges, any party may move for a pretrial conference under Article 39(a) to consider matters relating to government information that may arise in connection with the trial. Following such a motion, or when the military judge recognizes the need for such conference, the military judge must promptly hold a pretrial conference under Article 39(a).

(2) *Ex Parte Permissible.* Upon request by either party and with a showing of good cause, the military judge must hold such conference ex parte to the extent necessary to protect government information from disclosure.

(3) *Matters to be Established at Pretrial Conference.*

(A) *Timing of Subsequent Actions.* At the pretrial conference, the military judge must establish the timing of:

(i) requests for discovery;

(ii) the provision of notice required by subdivision (i) of this rule; and

(iii) the initiation of the procedure established by subdivision (j) of this rule.

(B) *Other Matters.* At the pretrial conference, the military judge may also consider any matter which relates to government information or which may promote a fair and expeditious trial.

(4) *Convening Authority Notice and Action.* If a claim of privilege has been made under this rule with respect to government information that apparently contains evidence that is relevant and necessary to an element of the offense or a legally cognizable defense and is otherwise admissible in evidence in the court-martial proceeding, the matter must be reported to the convening authority. The convening authority may:

(A) institute action to obtain the information for use by the military judge in making a determination under subdivision (j);

27

(B) dismiss the charges;

(C) dismiss the charges or specifications or both to which the information relates; or

(D) take such other action as may be required in the interests of justice.

(5) *Remedies.* If after a reasonable period of time the information is not provided to the military judge in circumstances where proceeding with the case without such information would materially prejudice a substantial right of the accused, the military judge must dismiss the charges or specifications or both to which the information relates.

(g) *Protective Orders.* Upon motion of the trial counsel, the military judge must issue an order to protect against the disclosure of any government information that has been disclosed by the United States to any accused in any court-martial proceeding or that has otherwise been provided to, or obtained by, any such accused in any such court-martial proceeding. The terms of any such protective order may include, but are not limited to, provisions:

(1) prohibiting the disclosure of the information except as authorized by the military judge;

(2) requiring storage of the material in a manner appropriate for the nature of the material to be disclosed;

(3) requiring controlled access to the material during normal business hours and at other times upon reasonable notice;

(4) requiring the maintenance of logs recording access by persons authorized by the military judge to have access to the government information in connection with the preparation of the defense;

(5) regulating the making and handling of notes taken from material containing government information; or

(6) requesting the convening authority to authorize the assignment of government security personnel and the provision of government storage facilities.

(h) *Discovery and Access by the Accused.*

(1) *Limitations.*

(A) *Government Claim of Privilege.* In a court-martial proceeding in which the government seeks to delete, withhold, or otherwise obtain other relief with respect to the discovery of or access to any government information subject to a claim of privilege, the trial counsel must submit a declaration invoking the United States' government information privilege and setting forth the detriment to the public interest that the discovery of or access to such information reasonably could be expected to cause. The declaration must be signed by a knowledgeable United States official as described in subdivision (d) of this rule.

(B) *Standard for Discovery or Access by the Accused.* Upon the submission of a declaration under subdivision (h)(1)(A), the military judge may not authorize the discovery of or access to such government information unless the military judge determines that such government information would be noncumulative, relevant, and helpful to a legally cognizable defense, rebuttal of the prosecution's case, or to sentencing. If the discovery of or access to such government information is authorized, it must be addressed in accordance with the requirements of subdivision (h)(2).

(2) *Alternatives to Full Disclosure.*

(A) *Substitutions and Other Alternatives.* The military judge, in assessing the accused's right to discover or access government information under subdivision (h), may authorize the government:

(i) to delete or withhold specified items of government information;

(ii) to substitute a summary for government information; or

(iii) to substitute a statement admitting relevant facts that the government information or material would tend to prove, unless the military judge determines that disclosure of the government information itself is necessary to enable the accused to prepare for trial.

(B) *In Camera Review.* The military judge must, upon the request of the prosecution, conduct an in camera review of the prosecution's motion and any materials submitted in support thereof and must not disclose such information to the accused.

(C) *Action by Military Judge.* The military judge must grant the request of the trial counsel to substitute a summary or to substitute a statement admitting relevant facts, or to provide other relief in accordance with subdivision (h)(2)(A), if the military judge finds that the summary, statement, or other relief would provide the accused with substantially the same ability to make a defense as would discovery of or access to the specific government information.

(i) *Disclosure by the Accused.*

(1) *Notification to Trial Counsel and Military Judge.* If an accused reasonably expects to disclose, or to cause the disclosure of, government information subject to a claim of privilege in any manner in connection with any trial or pretrial proceeding involving the prosecution of such accused, the accused must, within the time specified by the

28

military judge or, where no time is specified, prior to arraignment of the accused, notify the trial counsel and the military judge in writing.

(2) *Content of Notice.* Such notice must include a brief description of the government information.

(3) *Continuing Duty to Notify.* Whenever the accused learns of additional government information the accused reasonably expects to disclose, or to cause the disclosure of, at any such proceeding, the accused must notify trial counsel and the military judge in writing as soon as possible thereafter and must include a brief description of the government information.

(4) *Limitation on Disclosure by Accused.* The accused may not disclose, or cause the disclosure of, any information known or believed to be subject to a claim of privilege in connection with a trial or pretrial proceeding until:

(A) notice has been given under subdivision (i); and

(B) the government has been afforded a reasonable opportunity to seek a determination pursuant to the procedure set forth in subdivision (j).

(5) *Failure to Comply.* If the accused fails to comply with the requirements of subdivision (i), the military judge:

(A) may preclude disclosure of any government information not made the subject of notification; and

(B) may prohibit the examination by the accused of any witness with respect to any such information.

(j) *Procedure for Use of Government Information Subject to a Claim of Privilege in Trials and Pretrial Proceedings.*

(1) *Hearing on Use of Government Information.*

(A) *Motion for Hearing.* Within the time specified by the military judge for the filing of a motion under this rule, either party may move for an in camera hearing concerning the use at any proceeding of any government information that may be subject to a claim of privilege. Upon a request by either party, the military judge must conduct such a hearing and must rule prior to conducting any further proceedings.

(B) *Request for In Camera Hearing.* Any hearing held pursuant to subdivision (j) must be held in camera if a knowledgeable United States official described in subdivision (d) of this rule submits to the military judge a declaration that disclosure of the information reasonably could be expected to cause identifiable damage to the public interest.

(C) *Notice to Accused.* Subject to subdivision (j)(2) below, the prosecution must disclose government information claimed to be privileged under this rule for the limited purpose of litigating, in camera, the admissibility of the information at trial. The military judge must enter an appropriate protective order to the accused and all other appropriate trial participants concerning the disclosure of the information according to subdivision (g), above. The accused may not disclose any information provided under subdivision (j) unless, and until, such information has been admitted into evidence by the military judge. In the in camera hearing, both parties may have the opportunity to brief and argue the admissibility of the government information at trial.

(D) *Standard for Disclosure.* Government information is subject to disclosure at the court-martial proceeding under subdivision (j) if the party making the request demonstrates a specific need for information containing evidence that is relevant to the guilt or innocence or to punishment of the accused, and is otherwise admissible in the court-martial proceeding.

(E) *Written Findings.* As to each item of government information, the military judge must set forth in writing the basis for the determination.

(2) *Alternatives to Full Disclosure.*

(A) *Motion by the Prosecution.* Upon any determination by the military judge authorizing disclosure of specific government information under the procedures established by subdivision (j), the prosecution may move that, in lieu of the disclosure of such information, the military judge order:

(i)   the substitution for such government information of a statement admitting relevant facts that the specific government information would tend to prove;

(ii) the substitution for such government information of a summary of the specific government information; or

(iii) any other procedure or redaction limiting the disclosure of specific government information.

(B) *Hearing.* The military judge must hold a hearing on any motion under subdivision (j). At the request of the trial counsel, the military judge will conduct an in camera hearing.

29

(C) *Standard for Use of Alternatives.* The military judge must grant such a motion of the trial counsel if the military judge finds that the statement, summary, or other procedure or redaction will provide the accused with substantially the same ability to make his or her defense as would disclosure of the specific government information.

(3) *Sealing of Records of In Camera Hearings.* If at the close of an in camera hearing under subdivision (j) (or any portion of a hearing under subdivision (j) that is held in camera), the military judge determines that the government information at issue may not be disclosed or elicited at the trial or pretrial proceeding, the record of such in camera hearing must be sealed in accordance with R.C.M. 1103A and preserved for use in the event of an appeal. The accused may seek reconsideration of the military judge's determination prior to or during trial.

(4) *Remedies.*

(A) If the military judge determines that alternatives to full disclosure may not be used and the prosecution continues to object to disclosure of the information, the military judge must issue any order that the interests of justice require, including but not limited to, an order:

(i) striking or precluding all or part of the testimony of a witness;

(ii) declaring a mistrial;

(iii) finding against the government on any issue as to which the evidence is relevant and necessary to the defense;

(iv) dismissing the charges, with or without prejudice; or

(v) dismissing the charges or specifications or both to which the information relates.

(B) The government may avoid the sanction for nondisclosure by permitting the accused to disclose the information at the pertinent court-martial proceeding.

(5) *Disclosure of Rebuttal Information.* Whenever the military judge determines that government information may be disclosed in connection with a trial or pretrial proceeding, the military judge must, unless the interests of fairness do not so require, order the prosecution to provide the accused with the information it expects to use to rebut the government information.

(A) *Continuing Duty.* The military judge may place the prosecution under a continuing duty to disclose such rebuttal information.

(B) *Sanction for Failure to Comply.* If the prosecution fails to comply with its obligation under subdivision (j), the military judge may make such ruling as the interests of justice require, to include:

(i) excluding any evidence not made the subject of a required disclosure; and

(ii) prohibiting the examination by the prosecution of any witness with respect to such information.

(k) *Appeals of Orders and Rulings.* In a court-martial in which a punitive discharge may be adjudged, the government may appeal an order or ruling of the military judge that terminates the proceedings with respect to a charge or specification, directs the disclosure of government information, or imposes sanctions for nondisclosure of government information. The government may also appeal an order or ruling in which the military judge refuses to issue a protective order sought by the United States to prevent the disclosure of government information, or to enforce such an order previously issued by appropriate authority. The government may not appeal an order or ruling that is, or amounts to, a finding of not guilty with respect to the charge or specification.

(l) *Introduction into Evidence of Government Information Subject to a Claim of Privilege.*

(1) *Precautions.* The military judge in a trial by court-martial, in order to prevent unnecessary disclosure of government information after there has been a claim of privilege under this rule, may order admission into evidence of only part of a writing, recording, or photograph or admit into evidence the whole writing, recording, or photograph with excision of some or all of the government information contained therein, unless the whole ought in fairness to be considered.

(2) *Government Information Kept Under Seal.* The military judge must allow government information offered or accepted into evidence to remain under seal during the trial, even if such evidence is disclosed in the court-martial proceeding, and may, upon motion by the prosecution, seal exhibits containing government information in accordance with R.C.M. 1103A for any period after trial as necessary to prevent a disclosure of government information when a knowledgeable United States official described in subdivision (d) submits to the military judge a declaration setting forth the detriment to the public interest that the disclosure of such information reasonably could be expected to cause.

(3) *Testimony.*

(A) *Objection by Trial Counsel.* During examination of a witness, trial counsel may object to any question or line of inquiry that may require the witness to disclose government information not previously found admissible if such information has been or is reasonably likely to be the subject of a claim of privilege under this rule.

(B) *Action by Military Judge*. Following such an objection, the military judge must take such suitable action to determine whether the response is admissible as will safeguard against the compromise of any government information. Such action may include requiring trial counsel to provide the military judge with a proffer of the witness's response to the question or line of inquiry and requiring the accused to provide the military judge with a proffer of the nature of the information sought to be elicited by the accused. Upon request, the military judge may accept an ex parte proffer by trial counsel to the extent necessary to protect government information from disclosure.

(m) *Record of Trial*. If under this rule any information is withheld from the accused, the accused objects to such withholding, and the trial is continued to an adjudication of guilt of the accused, the entire unaltered text of the relevant documents as well as the prosecution's motion and any materials submitted in support thereof must be sealed in accordance with R.C.M. 1103A and attached to the record of trial as an appellate exhibit. Such material must be made available to reviewing authorities in closed proceedings for the purpose of reviewing the determination of the military judge.

Rule 507. Identity of Informants

(a) *General Rule*. The United States or a State or subdivision thereof has a privilege to refuse to disclose the identity of an informant. Unless otherwise privileged under these rules, the communications of an informant are not privileged except to the extent necessary to prevent the disclosure of the informant's identity.

(b) *Definitions*. As used in this rule:

(1) "Informant" means a person who has furnished information relating to or assisting in an investigation of a possible violation of law to a person whose official duties include the discovery, investigation, or prosecution of crime.

(2) "In camera review" means an inspection of documents or other evidence conducted by the military judge alone in chambers and not on the record.

(c) *Who May Claim the Privilege*. The privilege may be claimed by an appropriate representative of the United States, regardless of whether information was furnished to an officer of the United States or a State or subdivision thereof. The privilege may be claimed by an appropriate representative of a State or subdivision if the information was furnished to an officer thereof, except the privilege will not be allowed if the prosecution objects.

(d) *Exceptions*.

(1) *Voluntary Disclosures; Informant as a Prosecution Witness*. No privilege exists under this rule:

(A) if the identity of the informant has been disclosed to those who would have cause to resent the communication by a holder of the privilege or by the informant's own action; or

(B) if the informant appears as a witness for the prosecution.

(2) *Informant as a Defense Witness*. If a claim of privilege has been made under this rule, the military judge must, upon motion by the accused, determine whether disclosure of the identity of the informant is necessary to the accused's defense on the issue of guilt or innocence. Whether such a necessity exists will depend on the particular circumstances of each case, taking into consideration the offense charged, the possible defense, the possible significance of the informant's testimony, and other relevant factors. If it appears from the evidence in the case or from other showing by a party that an informant may be able to give testimony necessary to the accused's defense on the issue of guilt or innocence, the military judge may make any order required by the interests of justice.

(3) *Informant as a Witness regarding a Motion to Suppress Evidence*. If a claim of privilege has been made under this rule with respect to a motion under Mil. R. Evid. 311, the military judge must, upon motion of the accused, determine whether disclosure of the identity of the informant is required by the United States Constitution as applied to members of the armed forces. In making this determination, the military judge may make any order required by the interests of justice.

(e) *Procedures*.

(1) *In Camera Review*. If the accused has articulated a basis for disclosure under the standards set forth in this rule, the prosecution may ask the military judge to conduct an in camera review of affidavits or other evidence relevant to disclosure.

(2) *Order by the Military Judge*. If a claim of privilege has been made under this rule, the military judge may make any order required by the interests of justice.

(3) *Action by the Convening Authority*. If the military judge determines that disclosure of the identity of the informant is required under the standards set forth in this rule, and the prosecution elects not to disclose the identity of the informant, the matter must be reported to the convening authority. The convening authority may institute

31

action to secure disclosure of the identity of the informant, terminate the proceedings, or take such other action as may be appropriate under the circumstances.

(4) *Remedies.* If, after a reasonable period of time disclosure is not made, the military judge, sua sponte or upon motion of either counsel and after a hearing if requested by either party, may dismiss the charge or specifications or both to which the information regarding the informant would relate if the military judge determines that further proceedings would materially prejudice a substantial right of the accused.

Rule 508. Political Vote

A person has a privilege to refuse to disclose the tenor of the person's vote at a political election conducted by secret ballot unless the vote was cast illegally.

Rule 509. Deliberations of Courts and Juries

Except as provided in Mil. R. Evid. 606, the deliberations of courts, courts-martial, military judges, and grand and petit juries are privileged to the extent that such matters are privileged in trial of criminal cases in the United States district courts, but the results of the deliberations are not privileged.

Rule 510. Waiver of Privilege by Voluntary Disclosure

(a) A person upon whom these rules confer a privilege against disclosure of a confidential matter or communication waives the privilege if the person or the person's predecessor while holder of the privilege voluntarily discloses or consents to disclosure of any significant part of the matter or communication under such circumstances that it would be inappropriate to allow the claim of privilege. This rule does not apply if the disclosure is itself a privileged communication.

(b) Unless testifying voluntarily concerning a privileged matter or communication, an accused who testifies in his or her own behalf or a person who testifies under a grant or promise of immunity does not, merely by reason of testifying, waive a privilege to which he or she may be entitled pertaining to the confidential matter or communication.

Rule 511. Privileged Matter Disclosed Under Compulsion or Without Opportunity to Claim Privilege

(a) *General Rule.* Evidence of a statement or other disclosure of privileged matter is not admissible against the holder of the privilege if disclosure was compelled erroneously or was made without an opportunity for the holder of the privilege to claim the privilege.

(b) *Use of Communications Media.* The telephonic transmission of information otherwise privileged under these rules does not affect its privileged character. Use of electronic means of communication other than the telephone for transmission of information otherwise privileged under these rules does not affect the privileged character of such information if use of such means of communication is necessary and in furtherance of the communication.

Rule 512. Comment upon or Inference from Claim of Privilege; Instruction

(a) *Comment or Inference Not Permitted.*

(1) The claim of a privilege by the accused whether in the present proceeding or upon a prior occasion is not a proper subject of comment by the military judge or counsel for any party. No inference may be drawn therefrom.

(2) The claim of a privilege by a person other than the accused whether in the present proceeding or upon a prior occasion normally is not a proper subject of comment by the military judge or counsel for any party. An adverse inference may not be drawn therefrom except when determined by the military judge to be required by the interests of justice.

(b) *Claiming a Privilege Without the Knowledge of the Members.* In a trial before a court-martial with members, proceedings must be conducted, to the extent practicable, so as to facilitate the making of claims of privilege without the knowledge of the members. Subdivision (b) does not apply to a special court-martial without a military judge.

(c) *Instruction.* Upon request, any party against whom the members might draw an adverse inference from a claim of privilege is entitled to an instruction that no inference may be drawn therefrom except as provided in subdivision (a)(2).

32

Rule 513. Psychotherapist—Patient Privilege

(a) *General Rule.* A patient has a privilege to refuse to disclose and to prevent any other person from disclosing a confidential communication made between the patient and a psychotherapist or an assistant to the psychotherapist, in a case arising under the Uniform Code of Military Justice, if such communication was made for the purpose of facilitating diagnosis or treatment of the patient's mental or emotional condition.

(b) *Definitions.* As used in this rule:

(1) "Patient" means a person who consults with or is examined or interviewed by a psychotherapist for purposes of advice, diagnosis, or treatment of a mental or emotional condition.

(2) "Psychotherapist" means a psychiatrist, clinical psychologist, or clinical social worker who is licensed in any State, territory, possession, the District of Columbia or Puerto Rico to perform professional services as such, or who holds credentials to provide such services from any military health care facility, or is a person reasonably believed by the patient to have such license or credentials.

(3) "Assistant to a psychotherapist" means a person directed by or assigned to assist a psychotherapist in providing professional services, or is reasonably believed by the patient to be such.

(4) A communication is "confidential" if not intended to be disclosed to third persons other than those to whom disclosure is in furtherance of the rendition of professional services to the patient or those reasonably necessary for such transmission of the communication.

(5) "Evidence of a patient's records or communications" means testimony of a psychotherapist, or assistant to the same, or patient records that pertain to communications by a patient to a psychotherapist, or assistant to the same, for the purposes of diagnosis or treatment of the patient's mental or emotional condition.

(c) *Who May Claim the Privilege.* The privilege may be claimed by the patient or the guardian or conservator of the patient. A person who may claim the privilege may authorize trial counsel or defense counsel to claim the privilege on his or her behalf. The psychotherapist or assistant to the psychotherapist who received the communication may claim the privilege on behalf of the patient. The authority of such a psychotherapist, assistant, guardian, or conservator to so assert the privilege is presumed in the absence of evidence to the contrary.

(d) *Exceptions.* There is no privilege under this rule:

(1) when the patient is dead;

(2) when the communication is evidence of child abuse or of neglect, or in a proceeding in which one spouse is charged with a crime against a child of either spouse;

(3) when federal law, state law, or service regulation imposes a duty to report information contained in a communication;

(4) when a psychotherapist or assistant to a psychotherapist believes that a patient's mental or emotional condition makes the patient a danger to any person, including the patient;

(5) if the communication clearly contemplated the future commission of a fraud or crime or if the services of the psychotherapist are sought or obtained to enable or aid anyone to commit or plan to commit what the patient knew or reasonably should have known to be a crime or fraud;

(6) when necessary to ensure the safety and security of military personnel, military dependents, military property, classified information, or the accomplishment of a military mission;

(7) when an accused offers statements or other evidence concerning his mental condition in defense, extenuation, or mitigation, under circumstances not covered by R.C.M. 706 or Mil. R. Evid. 302. In such situations, the military judge may, upon motion, order disclosure of any statement made by the accused to a psychotherapist as may be necessary in the interests of justice; or

(8) when admission or disclosure of a communication is constitutionally required.

(e) *Procedure to Determine Admissibility of Patient Records or Communications.*

(1) In any case in which the production or admission of records or communications of a patient other than the accused is a matter in dispute, a party may seek an interlocutory ruling by the military judge. In order to obtain such a ruling, the party must:

(A) file a written motion at least 5 days prior to entry of pleas specifically describing the evidence and stating the purpose for which it is sought or offered, or objected to, unless the military judge, for good cause shown, requires a different time for filing or permits filing during trial; and

(B) serve the motion on the opposing party, the military judge and, if practical, notify the patient or the patient's guardian, conservator, or representative that the motion has been filed and that the patient has an opportunity to be heard as set forth in subdivision (e)(2).

33

(2) Before ordering the production or admission of evidence of a patient's records or communication, the military judge must conduct a hearing. Upon the motion of counsel for either party and upon good cause shown, the military judge may order the hearing closed. At the hearing, the parties may call witnesses, including the patient, and offer other relevant evidence. The patient must be afforded a reasonable opportunity to attend the hearing and be heard at the patient's own expense unless the patient has been otherwise subpoenaed or ordered to appear at the hearing. However, the proceedings may not be unduly delayed for this purpose. In a case before a court-martial composed of a military judge and members, the military judge must conduct the hearing outside the presence of the members.

(3) The military judge may examine the evidence or a proffer thereof in camera, if such examination is necessary to rule on the motion.

(4) To prevent unnecessary disclosure of evidence of a patient's records or communications, the military judge may issue protective orders or may admit only portions of the evidence.

(5) The motion, related papers, and the record of the hearing must be sealed in accordance with R.C.M. 1103A and must remain under seal unless the military judge or an appellate court orders otherwise.

Rule 514. Victim Advocate—Victim Privilege

(a) *General Rule.* A victim has a privilege to refuse to disclose and to prevent any other person from disclosing a confidential communication made between the alleged victim and a victim advocate, in a case arising under the Uniform Code of Military Justice, if such communication was made for the purpose of facilitating advice or supportive assistance to the alleged victim.

(b) *Definitions.* As used in this rule:

(1) "Victim" means any person who is alleged to have suffered direct physical or emotional harm as the result of a sexual or violent offense.

(2) "Victim advocate" means a person who:

(A) is designated in writing as a victim advocate in accordance with service regulation;

(B) is authorized to perform victim advocate duties in accordance with service regulation and is acting in the performance of those duties; or

(C) is certified as a victim advocate pursuant to federal or state requirements.

(3) A communication is "confidential" if made in the course of the victim advocate - victim relationship and not intended to be disclosed to third persons other than those to whom disclosure is made in furtherance of the rendition of advice or assistance to the alleged victim or those reasonably necessary for such transmission of the communication.

(4) "Evidence of a victim's records or communications" means testimony of a victim advocate, or records that pertain to communications by a victim to a victim advocate, for the purposes of advising or providing supportive assistance to the victim.

(c) *Who May Claim the Privilege.* The privilege may be claimed by the victim or the guardian or conservator of the victim. A person who may claim the privilege may authorize trial counsel or a defense counsel representing the victim to claim the privilege on his or her behalf. The victim advocate who received the communication may claim the privilege on behalf of the victim. The authority of such a victim advocate, guardian, conservator, or a defense counsel representing the victim to so assert the privilege is presumed in the absence of evidence to the contrary.

(d) *Exceptions.* There is no privilege under this rule:

(1) when the victim is dead;

(2) when federal law, state law, or service regulation imposes a duty to report information contained in a communication;

(3) when a victim advocate believes that a victim's mental or emotional condition makes the victim a danger to any person, including the victim;

(4) if the communication clearly contemplated the future commission of a fraud or crime, or if the services of the victim advocate are sought or obtained to enable or aid anyone to commit or plan to commit what the victim knew or reasonably should have known to be a crime or fraud;

(5) when necessary to ensure the safety and security of military personnel, military dependents, military property, classified information, or the accomplishment of a military mission; or

(6) when admission or disclosure of a communication is constitutionally required.

(e) *Procedure to Determine Admissibility of Victim Records or Communications.*

34

(1) In any case in which the production or admission of records or communications of a victim is a matter in dispute, a party may seek an interlocutory ruling by the military judge. In order to obtain such a ruling, the party must:

(A) file a written motion at least 5 days prior to entry of pleas specifically describing the evidence and stating the purpose for which it is sought or offered, or objected to, unless the military judge, for good cause shown, requires a different time for filing or permits filing during trial; and

(B) serve the motion on the opposing party, the military judge and, if practicable, notify the victim or the victim's guardian, conservator, or representative that the motion has been filed and that the victim has an opportunity to be heard as set forth in subdivision (e)(2).

(2) Before ordering the production or admission of evidence of a victim's records or communication, the military judge must conduct a hearing. Upon the motion of counsel for either party and upon good cause shown, the military judge may order the hearing closed. At the hearing, the parties may call witnesses, including the victim, and offer other relevant evidence. The victim must be afforded a reasonable opportunity to attend the hearing and be heard at the victim's own expense unless the victim has been otherwise subpoenaed or ordered to appear at the hearing. However, the proceedings may not be unduly delayed for this purpose. In a case before a court-martial composed of a military judge and members, the military judge must conduct the hearing outside the presence of the members.

(3) The military judge may examine the evidence or a proffer thereof in camera, if such examination is necessary to rule on the motion.

(4) To prevent unnecessary disclosure of evidence of a victim's records or communications, the military judge may issue protective orders or may admit only portions of the evidence.

(5) The motion, related papers, and the record of the hearing must be sealed in accordance with R.C.M. 1103A and must remain under seal unless the military judge or an appellate court orders otherwise.

Rule 601. Competency to Testify in General

Every person is competent to be a witness unless these rules provide otherwise.

Rule 602. Need for Personal Knowledge

A witness may testify to a matter only if evidence is introduced sufficient to support a finding that the witness has personal knowledge of the matter. Evidence to prove personal knowledge may consist of the witness's own testimony. This rule does not apply to a witness's expert testimony under Mil. R. Evid. 703.

Rule 603. Oath or Affirmation to Testify Truthfully

Before testifying, a witness must give an oath or affirmation to testify truthfully. It must be in a form designed to impress that duty on the witness's conscience.

Rule 604. Interpreter

An interpreter must be qualified and must give an oath or affirmation to make a true translation.

Rule 605. Military Judge's Competency as a Witness

(a) The presiding military judge may not testify as a witness at any proceeding of that court-martial. A party need not object to preserve the issue.

(b) This rule does not preclude the military judge from placing on the record matters concerning docketing of the case.

Rule 606. Member's Competency as a Witness

(a) *At the Trial by Court-Martial.* A member of a court-martial may not testify as a witness before the other members at any proceeding of that court-martial. If a member is called to testify, the military judge must – except in a special court-martial without a military judge –give the opposing party an opportunity to object outside the presence of the members.

(b) *During an Inquiry into the Validity of a Finding or Sentence.*

(1) *Prohibited Testimony or Other Evidence.* During an inquiry into the validity of a finding or sentence, a member of a court-martial may not testify about any statement made or incident that occurred during the

35

deliberations of that court-martial; the effect of anything on that member's or another member's vote; or any member's mental processes concerning the finding or sentence. The military judge may not receive a member's affidavit or evidence of a member's statement on these matters.

    (2) *Exceptions*. A member may testify about whether:

        (A) extraneous prejudicial information was improperly brought to the members' attention;

        (B) unlawful command influence or any other outside influence was improperly brought to bear on any member; or

        (C) a mistake was made in entering the finding or sentence on the finding or sentence forms.

Rule 607. Who May Impeach a Witness

Any party, including the party that called the witness, may attack the witness's credibility.

Rule 608. A Witness's Character for Truthfulness or Untruthfulness

(a) *Reputation or Opinion Evidence*. A witness's credibility may be attacked or supported by testimony about the witness's reputation for having a character for truthfulness or untruthfulness, or by testimony in the form of an opinion about that character. Evidence of truthful character is admissible only after the witness's character for truthfulness has been attacked.

(b) *Specific Instances of Conduct*. Except for a criminal conviction under Mil. R. Evid. 609, extrinsic evidence is not admissible to prove specific instances of a witness's conduct in order to attack or support the witness's character for truthfulness. The military judge may, on cross-examination, allow them to be inquired into if they are probative of the character for truthfulness or untruthfulness of:

    (1) the witness; or

    (2) another witness whose character the witness being cross-examined has testified about.

By testifying on another matter, a witness does not waive any privilege against self-incrimination for testimony that relates only to the witness's character for truthfulness.

(c) *Evidence of Bias*. Bias, prejudice, or any motive to misrepresent may be shown to impeach the witness either by examination of the witness or by evidence otherwise adduced.

Rule 609. Impeachment by Evidence of a Criminal Conviction

(a) *In General*. The following rules apply to attacking a witness's character for truthfulness by evidence of a criminal conviction:

    (1) For a crime that, in the convicting jurisdiction, was punishable by death, dishonorable discharge, or by imprisonment for more than one year, the evidence:

        (A) must be admitted, subject to Mil. R. Evid. 403, in a court-martial in which the witness is not the accused; and

        (B) must be admitted in a court-martial in which the witness is the accused, if the probative value of the evidence outweighs its prejudicial effect to that accused; and

    (2) For any crime regardless of the punishment, the evidence must be admitted if the court can readily determine that establishing the elements of the crime required proving – or the witness's admitting – a dishonest act or false statement.

    (3) In determining whether a crime tried by court-martial was punishable by death, dishonorable discharge, or imprisonment in excess of one year, the maximum punishment prescribed by the President under Article 56 at the time of the conviction applies without regard to whether the case was tried by general, special, or summary court-martial.

(b) *Limit on Using the Evidence After 10 Years*. Subdivision (b) applies if more than 10 years have passed since the witness's conviction or release from confinement for it, whichever is later. Evidence of the conviction is admissible only if:

    (1) its probative value, supported by specific facts and circumstances, substantially outweighs its prejudicial effect; and

    (2) the proponent gives an adverse party reasonable written notice of the intent to use it so that the party has a fair opportunity to contest its use.

(c) *Effect of a Pardon, Annulment, or Certificate of Rehabilitation*. Evidence of a conviction is not admissible if:

36

(1) the conviction has been the subject of a pardon, annulment, certificate of rehabilitation, or other equivalent procedure based on a finding that the person has been rehabilitated, and the person has not been convicted of a later crime punishable by death, dishonorable discharge, or imprisonment for more than one year; or

(2) the conviction has been the subject of a pardon, annulment, or other equivalent procedure based on a finding of innocence.

(d) *Juvenile Adjudications.* Evidence of a juvenile adjudication is admissible under this rule only if:

(1) the adjudication was of a witness other than the accused;

(2) an adult's conviction for that offense would be admissible to attack the adult's credibility; and

(3) admitting the evidence is necessary to fairly determine guilt or innocence.

(e) *Pendency of an Appeal.* A conviction that satisfies this rule is admissible even if an appeal is pending, except that a conviction by summary court-martial or special court-martial without a military judge may not be used for purposes of impeachment until review has been completed under Article 64 or Article 66, if applicable. Evidence of the pendency is also admissible.

(f) *Definition.* For purposes of this rule, there is a "conviction" in a court-martial case when a sentence has been adjudged.

Rule 610. Religious Beliefs or Opinions

Evidence of a witness's religious beliefs or opinions is not admissible to attack or support the witness's credibility.

Rule 611. Mode and Order of Examining Witnesses and Presenting Evidence

(a) *Control by the Military Judge; Purposes.* The military judge should exercise reasonable control over the mode and order of examining witnesses and presenting evidence so as to:

(1) make those procedures effective for determining the truth;

(2) avoid wasting time; and

(3) protect witnesses from harassment or undue embarrassment.

(b) *Scope of Cross-Examination.* Cross-examination should not go beyond the subject matter of the direct examination and matters affecting the witness's credibility. The military judge may allow inquiry into additional matters as if on direct examination.

(c) *Leading Questions.* Leading questions should not be used on direct examination except as necessary to develop the witness's testimony. Ordinarily, the military judge should allow leading questions:

(1) on cross-examination; and

(2) when a party calls a hostile witness or a witness identified with an adverse party.

(d) *Remote live testimony of a child.*

(1) In a case involving domestic violence or the abuse of a child, the military judge must, subject to the requirements of subdivision (d)(3) of this rule, allow a child victim or witness to testify from an area outside the courtroom as prescribed in R.C.M. 914A.

(2) *Definitions.* As used in this rule:

(A) "Child" means a person who is under the age of 16 at the time of his or her testimony.

(B) "Abuse of a child" means the physical or mental injury, sexual abuse or exploitation, or negligent treatment of a child.

(C) "Exploitation" means child pornography or child prostitution.

(D) "Negligent treatment" means the failure to provide, for reasons other than poverty, adequate food, clothing, shelter, or medical care so as to endanger seriously the physical health of the child.

(E) "Domestic violence" means an offense that has as an element the use, or attempted or threatened use of physical force against a person by a current or former spouse, parent, or guardian of the victim; by a person with whom the victim shares a child in common; by a person who is cohabiting with or has cohabited with the victim as a spouse, parent, or guardian; or by a person similarly situated to a spouse, parent, or guardian of the victim.

(3) Remote live testimony will be used only where the military judge makes the following three findings on the record:

(A) that it is necessary to protect the welfare of the particular child witness;

(B) that the child witness would be traumatized, not by the courtroom generally, but by the presence of the defendant; and

37

(C) that the emotional distress suffered by the child witness in the presence of the defendant is more than *de minimis*.

(4) Remote live testimony of a child will not be used when the accused elects to absent himself from the courtroom in accordance with R.C.M. 804(d).

(5) In making a determination under subdivision (d)(3), the military judge may question the child in chambers, or at some comfortable place other than the courtroom, on the record for a reasonable period of time, in the presence of the child, a representative of the prosecution, a representative of the defense, and the child's attorney or guardian ad litem.

Rule 612. Writing Used to Refresh a Witness's Memory

(a) *Scope.* This rule gives an adverse party certain options when a witness uses a writing to refresh memory:

(1) while testifying; or

(2) before testifying, if the military judge decides that justice requires the party to have those options.

(b) *Adverse Party's Options; Deleting Unrelated Matter.* An adverse party is entitled to have the writing produced at the hearing, to inspect it, to cross-examine the witness about it, and to introduce in evidence any portion that relates to the witness's testimony. If the producing party claims that the writing includes unrelated or privileged matter, the military judge must examine the writing in camera, delete any unrelated or privileged portion, and order that the rest be delivered to the adverse party. Any portion deleted over objection must be preserved for the record.

(c) *Failure to Produce or Deliver the Writing.* If a writing is not produced or is not delivered as ordered, the military judge may issue any appropriate order. If the prosecution does not comply, the military judge must strike the witness's testimony or – if justice so requires – declare a mistrial.

(d) *No Effect on Other Disclosure Requirements.* This rule does not preclude disclosure of information required to be disclosed under other provisions of these rules or this Manual.

Rule 613. Witness's Prior Statement

(a) *Showing or Disclosing the Statement During Examination.* When examining a witness about the witness's prior statement, a party need not show it or disclose its contents to the witness. The party must, on request, show it or disclose its contents to an adverse party's attorney.

(b) *Extrinsic Evidence of a Prior Inconsistent Statement.* Extrinsic evidence of a witness's prior inconsistent statement is admissible only if the witness is given an opportunity to explain or deny the statement and an adverse party is given an opportunity to examine the witness about it, or if justice so requires. Subdivision (b) does not apply to an opposing party's statement under Mil R. Evid. 801(d)(2).

Rule 614. Court-Martial's Calling or Examining a Witness

(a) *Calling.* The military judge may – sua sponte or at the request of the members or the suggestion of a party – call a witness. Each party is entitled to cross-examine the witness. When the members wish to call or recall a witness, the military judge must determine whether the testimony would be relevant and not barred by any rule or provision of this Manual.

(b) *Examining.* The military judge or members may examine a witness regardless of who calls the witness. Members must submit their questions to the military judge in writing. Following the opportunity for review by both parties, the military judge must rule on the propriety of the questions, and ask the questions in an acceptable form on behalf of the members. When the military judge or the members call a witness who has not previously testified, the military judge may conduct the direct examination or may assign the responsibility to counsel for any party.

(c) *Objections.* A party may object to the court-martial's calling or examining a witness either at that time or at the next opportunity when the members are not present.

Rule 615. Excluding Witnesses

At a party's request, the military judge must order witnesses excluded so that they cannot hear other witnesses' testimony, or the military judge may do so *sua sponte*. This rule does not authorize excluding:

(a) the accused;

(b) a member of an armed service or an employee of the United States after being designated as a representative of the United States by the trial counsel;

(c) a person whose presence a party shows to be essential to presenting the party's case;

38

(d) a person authorized by statute to be present; or

(e) a victim of an offense from the trial of an accused for that offense, when the sole basis for exclusion would be that the victim may testify or present information during the presentencing phase of the trial.

Rule 701. Opinion Testimony by Lay Witnesses

If a witness is not testifying as an expert, testimony in the form of an opinion is limited to one that is:

(a) rationally based on the witness's perception;

(b) helpful to clearly understanding the witness's testimony or to determining a fact in issue; and

(c) not based on scientific, technical, or other specialized knowledge within the scope of Mil. R. Evid. 702.

Rule 702. Testimony by Expert Witnesses

A witness who is qualified as an expert by knowledge, skill, experience, training, or education may testify in the form of an opinion or otherwise if:

(a) the expert's scientific, technical, or other specialized knowledge will help the trier of fact to understand the evidence or to determine a fact in issue;

(b) the testimony is based on sufficient facts or data;

(c) the testimony is the product of reliable principles and methods; and

(d) the expert has reliably applied the principles and methods to the facts of the case.

Rule 703. Bases of an Expert's Opinion Testimony

An expert may base an opinion on facts or data in the case that the expert has been made aware of or personally observed. If experts in the particular field would reasonably rely on those kinds of facts or data in forming an opinion on the subject, they need not be admissible for the opinion to be admitted. If the facts or data would otherwise be inadmissible, the proponent of the opinion may disclose them to the members of a court-martial only if the military judge finds that their probative value in helping the members evaluate the opinion substantially outweighs their prejudicial effect.

Rule 704. Opinion on an Ultimate Issue

An opinion is not objectionable just because it embraces an ultimate issue.

Rule 705. Disclosing the Facts or Data Underlying an Expert's Opinion

Unless the military judge orders otherwise, an expert may state an opinion – and give the reasons for it – without first testifying to the underlying facts or data. The expert may be required to disclose those facts or data on cross-examination.

Rule 706. Court-Appointed Expert Witnesses

(a) *Appointment Process.* The trial counsel, the defense counsel, and the court-martial have equal opportunity to obtain expert witnesses under Article 46 and R.C.M. 703.

(b) *Compensation.* The compensation of expert witnesses is governed by R.C.M. 703.

(c) *Accused's Choice of Experts.* This rule does not limit an accused in calling any expert at the accused's own expense.

Rule 707. Polygraph Examinations

(a) *Prohibitions.* Notwithstanding any other provision of law, the result of a polygraph examination, the polygraph examiner's opinion, or any reference to an offer to take, failure to take, or taking of a polygraph examination is not admissible.

(b) *Statements Made During a Polygraph Examination.* This rule does not prohibit admission of an otherwise admissible statement made during a polygraph examination.

Rule 801. Definitions that Apply to this Section; Exclusions from Hearsay

(a) *Statement.* "Statement" means a person's oral assertion, written assertion, or nonverbal conduct, if the person intended it as an assertion.

39

(b) *Declarant.* "Declarant" means the person who made the statement.

(c) *Hearsay.* "Hearsay" means a statement that:

(1) the declarant does not make while testifying at the current trial or hearing; and

(2) a party offers in evidence to prove the truth of the matter asserted in the statement.

(d) *Statements that Are Not Hearsay.* A statement that meets the following conditions is not hearsay:

(1) *A Declarant-Witness's Prior Statement.* The declarant testifies and is subject to cross-examination about a prior statement, and the statement:

(A) is inconsistent with the declarant's testimony and was given under penalty of perjury at a trial, hearing, or other proceeding or in a deposition;

(B) is consistent with the declarant's testimony and is offered to rebut an express or implied charge that the declarant recently fabricated it or acted from a recent improper influence or motive in so testifying; or

(C) identifies a person as someone the declarant perceived earlier.

(2) *An Opposing Party's Statement.* The statement is offered against an opposing party and:

(A) was made by the party in an individual or representative capacity;

(B) is one the party manifested that it adopted or believed to be true;

(C) was made by a person whom the party authorized to make a statement on the subject;

(D) was made by the party's agent or employee on a matter within the scope of that relationship and while it existed; or

(E) was made by the party's co-conspirator during and in furtherance of the conspiracy.

The statement must be considered but does not by itself establish the declarant's authority under (C); the existence or scope of the relationship under (D); or the existence of the conspiracy or participation in it under (E).

Rule 802. The Rule against Hearsay

Hearsay is not admissible unless any of the following provides otherwise:

(a) a federal statute applicable in trial by courts-martial; or

(b) these rules.

Rule 803. Exceptions to the Rule against Hearsay – Regardless of Whether the Declarant Is Available as a Witness

The following are not excluded by the rule against hearsay, regardless of whether the declarant is available as a witness:

(1) *Present Sense Impression.* A statement describing or explaining an event or condition, made while or immediately after the declarant perceived it.

(2) *Excited Utterance.* A statement relating to a startling event or condition, made while the declarant was under the stress of excitement that it caused.

(3) *Then-Existing Mental, Emotional, or Physical Condition.* A statement of the declarant's then-existing state of mind (such as motive, intent, or plan) or emotional, sensory, or physical condition (such as mental feeling, pain, or bodily health), but not including a statement of memory or belief to prove the fact remembered or believed unless it relates to the validity or terms of the declarant's will.

(4) *Statement Made for Medical Diagnosis or Treatment.* A statement that –

(A) is made for – and is reasonably pertinent to – medical diagnosis or treatment; and

(B) describes medical history; past or present symptoms or sensations; their inception; or their general cause.

(5) *Recorded Recollection.* A record that:

(A) is on a matter the witness once knew about but now cannot recall well enough to testify fully and accurately;

(B) was made or adopted by the witness when the matter was fresh in the witness's memory; and

(C) accurately reflects the witness's knowledge.

If admitted, the record may be read into evidence but may be received as an exhibit only if offered by an adverse party.

(6) *Records of a Regularly Conducted Activity.* A record of an act, event, condition, opinion, or diagnosis if:

(A) the record was made at or near the time by – or from information transmitted by – someone with knowledge;

40

(B) the record was kept in the course of a regularly conducted activity of a uniformed service, business, institution, association, profession, organization, occupation, or calling of any kind, whether or not conducted for profit;

(C) making the record was a regular practice of that activity;

(D) all these conditions are shown by the testimony of the custodian or another qualified witness, or by a certification that complies with Mil. R. Evid. 902(11) or with a statute permitting certification in a criminal proceeding in a court of the United States; and

(E) neither the source of information nor the method or circumstances of preparation indicate a lack of trustworthiness.

Records of regularly conducted activities include, but are not limited to, enlistment papers, physical examination papers, fingerprint cards, forensic laboratory reports, chain of custody documents, morning reports and other personnel accountability documents, service records, officer and enlisted qualification records, logs, unit personnel diaries, individual equipment records, daily strength records of prisoners, and rosters of prisoners.

(7) *Absence of a Record of a Regularly Conducted Activity.* Evidence that a matter is not included in a record described in paragraph (6) if:

(A) the evidence is admitted to prove that the matter did not occur or exist;

(B) a record was regularly kept for a matter of that kind; and

(C) neither the possible source of the information nor other circumstances indicate a lack of trustworthiness.

(8) *Public Records.* A record or statement of a public office if:

(A) it sets out:

(i) the office's activities;

(ii) a matter observed while under a legal duty to report, but not including a matter observed by law-enforcement personnel and other personnel acting in a law enforcement capacity; or

(iii) against the government, factual findings from a legally authorized investigation; and

(B) neither the source of information nor other circumstances indicate a lack of trustworthiness.

Notwithstanding subdivision (8)(A)(ii), the following are admissible as a record of a fact or event if made by a person within the scope of the person's official duties and those duties included a duty to know or to ascertain through appropriate and trustworthy channels of information the truth of the fact or event and to record such fact or event: enlistment papers, physical examination papers, fingerprint cards, forensic laboratory reports, chain of custody documents, morning reports and other personnel accountability documents, service records, officer and enlisted qualification records, court-martial conviction records, logs, unit personnel diaries, individual equipment records, daily strength records of prisoners, and rosters of prisoners.

(9) *Public Records of Vital Statistics.* A record of a birth, death, or marriage, if reported to a public office in accordance with a legal duty.

(10) *Absence of a Public Record.* Testimony – or a certification under Mil. R. Evid. 902 – that a diligent search failed to disclose a public record or statement if the testimony or certification is admitted to prove that:

(A) the record or statement does not exist; or

(B) a matter did not occur or exist, if a public office regularly kept a record or statement for a matter of that kind.

(11) *Records of Religious Organizations Concerning Personal or Family History.* A statement of birth, legitimacy, ancestry, marriage, divorce, death, relationship by blood or marriage, or similar facts of personal or family history, contained in a regularly kept record of a religious organization.

(12) *Certificates of Marriage, Baptism, and Similar Ceremonies.* A statement of fact contained in a certificate:

(A) made by a person who is authorized by a religious organization or by law to perform the act certified;

(B) attesting that the person performed a marriage or similar ceremony or administered a sacrament; and

(C) purporting to have been issued at the time of the act or within a reasonable time after it.

(13) *Family Records.* A statement of fact about personal or family history contained in a family record, such as a Bible, genealogy, chart, engraving on a ring, inscription on a portrait, or engraving on an urn or burial marker.

(14) *Records of Documents that Affect an Interest in Property.* The record of a document that purports to establish or affect an interest in property if:

(A) the record is admitted to prove the content of the original recorded document, along with its signing and its delivery by each person who purports to have signed it;

(B) the record is kept in a public office; and

41

(C) a statute authorizes recording documents of that kind in that office.

(15) *Statements in Documents that Affect an Interest in Property*. A statement contained in a document that purports to establish or affect an interest in property if the matter stated was relevant to the document's purpose unless later dealings with the property are inconsistent with the truth of the statement or the purport of the document.

(16) *Statements in Ancient Documents*. A statement in a document that is at least 20 years old and whose authenticity is established.

(17) *Market Reports and Similar Commercial Publications*. Market quotations, lists (including government price lists), directories, or other compilations that are generally relied on by the public or by persons in particular occupations.

(18) *Statements in Learned Treatises, Periodicals, or Pamphlets*. A statement contained in a treatise, periodical, or pamphlet if:

　　(A) the statement is called to the attention of an expert witness on cross-examination or relied on by the expert on direct examination; and

　　(B) the publication is established as a reliable authority by the expert's admission or testimony, by another expert's testimony, or by judicial notice.

If admitted, the statement may be read into evidence but not received as an exhibit.

(19) *Reputation Concerning Personal or Family History*. A reputation among a person's family by blood, adoption, or marriage – or among a person's associates or in the community – concerning the person's birth, adoption, legitimacy, ancestry, marriage, divorce, death, relationship by blood, adoption, or marriage, or similar facts of personal or family history.

(20) *Reputation Concerning Boundaries or General History*. A reputation in a community – arising before the controversy – concerning boundaries of land in the community or customs that affect the land, or concerning general historical events important to that community, State, or nation.

(21) *Reputation Concerning Character*. A reputation among a person's associates or in the community concerning the person's character.

(22) *Judgment of a Previous Conviction*. Evidence of a final judgment of conviction if:

　　(A) the judgment was entered after a trial or guilty plea, but not a nolo contendere plea;

　　(B) the conviction was for a crime punishable by death, dishonorable discharge, or by imprisonment for more than a year;

　　(C) the evidence is admitted to prove any fact essential to the judgment; and

　　(D) when offered by the prosecutor for a purpose other than impeachment, the judgment was against the accused.

The pendency of an appeal may be shown but does not affect admissibility. In determining whether a crime tried by court-martial was punishable by death, dishonorable discharge, or imprisonment for more than one year, the maximum punishment prescribed by the President under Article 56 of the Uniform of Military Justice at the time of the conviction applies without regard to whether the case was tried by general, special, or summary court-martial.

(23) *Judgments Involving Personal, Family, or General History, or a Boundary*. A judgment that is admitted to prove a matter of personal, family, or general history, or boundaries, if the matter:

　　(A) was essential to the judgment; and

　　(B) could be proved by evidence of reputation.

Rule 804. Exceptions to the Rule Against Hearsay – When the Declarant Is Unavailable as a Witness

(a) *Criteria for Being Unavailable*. A declarant is considered to be unavailable as a witness if the declarant:

　　(1) is exempted from testifying about the subject matter of the declarant's statement because the military judge rules that a privilege applies;

　　(2) refuses to testify about the subject matter despite the military judge's order to do so;

　　(3) testifies to not remembering the subject matter;

　　(4) cannot be present or testify at the trial or hearing because of death or a then-existing infirmity, physical illness, or mental illness; or

　　(5) is absent from the trial or hearing and the statement's proponent has not been able, by process or other reasonable means, to procure:

　　　　(A) the declarant's attendance, in the case of a hearsay exception under subdivision (b)(1) or (b)(5);

42

(B) the declarant's attendance or testimony, in the case of a hearsay exception under subdivision (b)(2), (b)(3), or (b)(4); or

(6) is unavailable within the meaning of Article 49(d)(2).

Subdivision (a) does not apply if the statement's proponent procured or wrongfully caused the declarant's unavailability as a witness in order to prevent the declarant from attending or testifying.

(b) *The Exceptions.* The following are exceptions to the rule against hearsay, and are not excluded by that rule if the declarant is unavailable as a witness:

(1) *Former Testimony.* Testimony that:

(A) was given by a witness at a trial, hearing, or lawful deposition, whether given during the current proceeding or a different one; and

(B) is now offered against a party who had an opportunity and similar motive to develop it by direct, cross-, or redirect examination.

Subject to the limitations in Articles 49 and 50, a record of testimony given before a court-martial, court of inquiry, military commission, other military tribunal, or pretrial investigation under Article 32 is admissible under subdivision (b)(1) if the record of the testimony is a verbatim record.

(2) *Statement under the Belief of Imminent Death.* In a prosecution for any offense resulting in the death of the alleged victim, a statement that the declarant, while believing the declarant's death to be imminent, made about its cause or circumstances.

(3) *Statement against Interest.* A statement that:

(A) a reasonable person in the declarant's position would have made only if the person believed it to be true because, when made, it was so contrary to the declarant's proprietary or pecuniary interest or had so great a tendency to invalidate the declarant's claim against someone else or to expose the declarant to civil or criminal liability; and

(B) is supported by corroborating circumstances that clearly indicate its trustworthiness, if it tends to expose the declarant to criminal liability and is offered to exculpate the accused.

(4) *Statement of Personal or Family History.* A statement about:

(A) the declarant's own birth, adoption, legitimacy, ancestry, marriage, divorce, relationship by blood or marriage, or similar facts of personal or family history, even though the declarant had no way of acquiring personal knowledge about that fact; or

(B) another person concerning any of these facts, as well as death, if the declarant was related to the person by blood, adoption, or marriage or was so intimately associated with the person's family that the declarant's information is likely to be accurate.

(5) *Other Exceptions.* [Transferred to Mil.R.Evid. 807]

(6) *Statement Offered against a Party that Wrongfully Caused the Declarant's Unavailability.* A statement offered against a party that wrongfully caused or acquiesced in wrongfully causing the declarant's unavailability as a witness, and did so intending that result.

Rule 805. Hearsay Within Hearsay

Hearsay within hearsay is not excluded by the rule against hearsay if each part of the combined statements conforms with an exception or exclusion to the rule.

Rule 806. Attacking and Supporting the Declarant's Credibility

When a hearsay statement – or a statement described in Mil. R. Evid. 801(d)(2)(C), (D), or (E) – has been admitted in evidence, the declarant's credibility may be attacked, and then supported, by any evidence that would be admissible for those purposes if the declarant had testified as a witness. The military judge may admit evidence of the declarant's inconsistent statement or conduct, regardless of when it occurred or whether the declarant had an opportunity to explain or deny it. If the party against whom the statement was admitted calls the declarant as a witness, the party may examine the declarant on the statement as if on cross-examination.

Rule 807. Residual Exception

(a) *In General.* Under the following circumstances, a hearsay statement is not excluded by the rule against hearsay even if the statement is not specifically covered by a hearsay exception in Mil. R. Evid. 803 or 804:

(1) the statement has equivalent circumstantial guarantees of trustworthiness;

(2) it is offered as evidence of a material fact;

43

(3) it is more probative on the point for which it is offered than any other evidence that the proponent can obtain through reasonable efforts; and

(4) admitting it will best serve the purposes of these rules and the interests of justice.

(b) *Notice.* The statement is admissible only if, before the trial or hearing, the proponent gives an adverse party reasonable notice of the intent to offer the statement and its particulars, including the declarant's name and address, so that the party has a fair opportunity to meet it.

Rule 901. Authenticating or Identifying Evidence

(a) *In General.* To satisfy the requirement of authenticating or identifying an item of evidence, the proponent must produce evidence sufficient to support a finding that the item is what the proponent claims it is.

(b) *Examples.* The following are examples only – not a complete list – of evidence that satisfies the requirement:

(1) *Testimony of a Witness with Knowledge.* Testimony that an item is what it is claimed to be.

(2) *Nonexpert Opinion about Handwriting.* A nonexpert's opinion that handwriting is genuine, based on a familiarity with it that was not acquired for the current litigation.

(3) *Comparison by an Expert Witness or the Trier of Fact.* A comparison with an authenticated specimen by an expert witness or the trier of fact.

(4) *Distinctive Characteristics and the Like.* The appearance, contents, substance, internal patterns, or other distinctive characteristics of the item, taken together with all the circumstances.

(5) *Opinion about a Voice.* An opinion identifying a person's voice -- whether heard firsthand or through mechanical or electronic transmission or recording -- based on hearing the voice at any time under circumstances that connect it with the alleged speaker.

(6) *Evidence about a Telephone Conversation.* For a telephone conversation, evidence that a call was made to the number assigned at the time to:

(A) a particular person, if circumstances, including self-identification, show that the person answering was the one called; or

(B) a particular business, if the call was made to a business and the call related to business reasonably transacted over the telephone.

(7) *Evidence about Public Records.* Evidence that:

(A) a document was recorded or filed in a public office as authorized by law; or

(B) a purported public record or statement is from the office where items of this kind are kept.

(8) *Evidence about Ancient Documents or Data Compilations.* For a document or data compilation, evidence that it:

(A) is in a condition that creates no suspicion about its authenticity;

(B) was in a place where, if authentic, it would likely be; and

(C) is at least 20 years old when offered.

(9) *Evidence about a Process or System.* Evidence describing a process or system and showing that it produces an accurate result.

(10) *Methods Provided by a Statute or Rule.* Any method of authentication or identification allowed by a federal statute, a rule prescribed by the Supreme Court, or an applicable regulation prescribed pursuant to statutory authority.

Rule 902. Evidence that Is Self-Authenticating

The following items of evidence are self-authenticating; they require no extrinsic evidence of authenticity in order to be admitted:

(1) *Domestic Public Documents that are Sealed and Signed.* A document that bears:

(A) a seal purporting to be that of the United States; any State, district, Commonwealth, territory, or insular possession of the United States; the former Panama Canal Zone; the Trust Territory of the Pacific Islands; a political subdivision of any of these entities; or a department, agency, or officer of any entity named above; and

(B) a signature purporting to be an execution or attestation.

(2) *Domestic Public Documents that are Not Sealed but are Signed and Certified.* A document that bears no seal if:

(A) it bears the signature of an officer or employee of an entity named in subdivision (1)(A) above; and

44

(B) another public officer who has a seal and official duties within that same entity certifies under seal – or its equivalent – that the signer has the official capacity and that the signature is genuine.

(3) *Foreign Public Documents.* A document that purports to be signed or attested by a person who is authorized by a foreign country's law to do so. The document must be accompanied by a final certification that certifies the genuineness of the signature and official position of the signer or attester – or of any foreign official whose certificate of genuineness relates to the signature or attestation or is in a chain of certificates of genuineness relating to the signature or attestation. The certification may be made by a secretary of a United States embassy or legation; by a consul general, vice consul, or consular agent of the United States; or by a diplomatic or consular official of the foreign country assigned or accredited to the United States. If all parties have been given a reasonable opportunity to investigate the document's authenticity and accuracy, the military judge may, for good cause, either:

(A) order that it be treated as presumptively authentic without final certification; or

(B) allow it to be evidenced by an attested summary with or without final certification.

(4) *Certified Copies of Public Records.* A copy of an official record -- or a copy of a document that was recorded or filed in a public office as authorized by law -- if the copy is certified as correct by:

(A) the custodian or another person authorized to make the certification; or

(B) a certificate that complies with subdivision (1), (2), or (3) above, a federal statute, a rule prescribed by the Supreme Court, or an applicable regulation prescribed pursuant to statutory authority.

(4a) *Documents or Records of the United States Accompanied by Attesting Certificates.* Documents or records kept under the authority of the United States by any department, bureau, agency, office, or court thereof when attached to or accompanied by an attesting certificate of the custodian of the document or record without further authentication.

(5) *Official Publications.* A book, pamphlet, or other publication purporting to be issued by a public authority.

(6) *Newspapers and Periodicals.* Printed material purporting to be a newspaper or periodical.

(7) *Trade Inscriptions and the Like.* An inscription, sign, tag, or label purporting to have been affixed in the course of business and indicating origin, ownership, or control.

(8) *Acknowledged Documents.* A document accompanied by a certificate of acknowledgment that is lawfully executed by a notary public or another officer who is authorized to take acknowledgments.

(9) *Commercial Paper and Related Documents.* Commercial paper, a signature on it, and related documents, to the extent allowed by general commercial law.

(10) *Presumptions under a Federal Statute or Regulation.* A signature, document, or anything else that a federal statute, or an applicable regulation prescribed pursuant to statutory authority, declares to be presumptively or prima facie genuine or authentic.

(11) *Certified Domestic Records of a Regularly Conducted Activity.* The original or a copy of a domestic record that meets the requirements of Mil. R. Evid. 803(6)(A)-(C), as shown by a certification of the custodian or another qualified person that complies with a federal statute or a rule prescribed by the Supreme Court. Before the trial or hearing, or at a later time that the military judge allows for good cause, the proponent must give an adverse party reasonable written notice of the intent to offer the record and must make the record and certification available for inspection so that the party has a fair opportunity to challenge them.

Rule 903. Subscribing Witness's Testimony

A subscribing witness's testimony is necessary to authenticate a writing only if required by the law of the jurisdiction that governs its validity.

Rule 1001. Definitions That Apply to This Section

In this section:

(a) A "writing" consists of letters, words, numbers, or their equivalent set down in any form.

(b) A "recording" consists of letters, words, numbers, or their equivalent recorded in any manner.

(c) A "photograph" means a photographic image or its equivalent stored in any form.

(d) An "original" of a writing or recording means the writing or recording itself or any counterpart intended to have the same effect by the person who executed or issued it. For electronically stored information, "original" means any printout or other output readable by sight if it accurately reflects the information. An "original" of a photograph includes the negative or a print from it.

(e) A "duplicate" means a counterpart produced by a mechanical, photographic, chemical, electronic, or other equivalent process or technique that accurately reproduces the original.

45

Rule 1002. Requirement of the Original

An original writing, recording, or photograph is required in order to prove its content unless these rules, this Manual, or a federal statute provides otherwise.

Rule 1003. Admissibility of Duplicates

A duplicate is admissible to the same extent as the original unless a genuine question is raised about the original's authenticity or the circumstances make it unfair to admit the duplicate.

Rule 1004. Admissibility of Other Evidence of Content

An original is not required and other evidence of the content of a writing, recording, or photograph is admissible if:
(a) all the originals are lost or destroyed, and not by the proponent acting in bad faith;
(b) an original cannot be obtained by any available judicial process;
(c) the party against whom the original would be offered had control of the original; was at that time put on notice, by pleadings or otherwise, that the original would be a subject of proof at the trial or hearing; and fails to produce it at the trial or hearing; or
(d) the writing, recording, or photograph is not closely related to a controlling issue.

Rule 1005. Copies of Public Records to Prove Content

The proponent may use a copy to prove the content of an official record – or of a document that was recorded or filed in a public office as authorized by law – if these conditions are met: the record or document is otherwise admissible; and the copy is certified as correct in accordance with Mil. R. Evid. 902(4) or is testified to be correct by a witness who has compared it with the original. If no such copy can be obtained by reasonable diligence, then the proponent may use other evidence to prove the content.

Rule 1006. Summaries to Prove Content

The proponent may use a summary, chart, or calculation to prove the content of voluminous writings, recordings, or photographs that cannot be conveniently examined in court. The proponent must make the originals or duplicates available for examination or copying, or both, by other parties at a reasonable time or place. The military judge may order the proponent to produce them in court.

Rule 1007. Testimony or Statement of a Party to Prove Content

The proponent may prove the content of a writing, recording, or photograph by the testimony, deposition, or written statement of the party against whom the evidence is offered. The proponent need not account for the original.

Rule 1008. Functions of the Military Judge and the Members

Ordinarily, the military judge determines whether the proponent has fulfilled the factual conditions for admitting other evidence of the content of a writing, recording, or photograph under Mil. R. Evid. 1004 or 1005. When a court-martial is composed of a military judge and members, the members determine – in accordance with Mil. R. Evid. 104(b) – any issue about whether:
(a) an asserted writing, recording, or photograph ever existed;
(b) another one produced at the trial or hearing is the original; or
(c) other evidence of content accurately reflects the content.

Rule 1101. Applicability of these Rules

(a) *In General.* Except as otherwise provided in this Manual, these rules apply generally to all courts-martial, including summary courts-martial, Article 39(a) sessions, limited factfinding proceedings ordered on review, proceedings in revision, and contempt proceedings other than contempt proceedings in which the judge may act summarily.
(b) *Rules Relaxed.* The application of these rules may be relaxed in presentencing proceedings as provided under R.C.M. 1001 and otherwise as provided in this Manual.
(c) *Rules on Privilege.* The rules on privilege apply at all stages of a case or proceeding.
(d) *Exceptions.* These rules – except for Mil. R. Evid. 412 and those on privilege – do not apply to the following:

46

(1) the military judge's determination, under Rule 104(a), on a preliminary question of fact governing admissibility;

(2) pretrial investigations under Article 32;

(3) proceedings for vacation of suspension of sentence under Article 72; and

(4) miscellaneous actions and proceedings related to search authorizations, pretrial restraint, pretrial confinement, or other proceedings authorized under the Uniform Code of Military Justice or this Manual that are not listed in subdivision (a).

Rule 1102. Amendments

(a) *General Rule.* Amendments to the Federal Rules of Evidence – other than Articles III and V – will amend parallel provisions of the Military Rules of Evidence by operation of law 18 months after the effective date of such amendments, unless action to the contrary is taken by the President.

(b) *Rules Determined Not to Apply.* The President has determined that the following Federal Rules of Evidence do not apply to the Military Rules of Evidence: Rules 301, 302, 415, and 902(12).

Rule 1103. Title

These rules may be cited as the Military Rules of Evidence.

Sec. 2. Part IV of the Manual for Courts-Martial, United States, is amended as follows:

(a) Paragraph 45, Article 120, Rape and sexual assault generally, subparagraph e is amended to read as follows:

"e. *Maximum punishment.*

(1) *Rape.* Dishonorable discharge, forfeiture of all pay and allowances, and confinement for life without eligibility for parole.

(2) *Sexual assault.* Dishonorable discharge, forfeiture of all pay and allowances, and confinement for 30 years.

(3) *Aggravated sexual contact.* Dishonorable discharge, forfeiture of all pay and allowances, and confinement for 20 years.

(4) *Abusive sexual contact.* Dishonorable discharge, forfeiture of all pay and allowances, and confinement for 7 years."

(b) Paragraph 45b, Article 120b, Rape and sexual assault of a child, is amended by inserting the following new subparagraph e:

"e. *Maximum punishment.*

(1) *Rape of a child.* Dishonorable discharge, forfeiture of all pay and allowances, and confinement for life without eligibility for parole.

(2) *Sexual assault of a child.* Dishonorable discharge, forfeiture of all pay and allowances, and confinement for 30 years.

(3) *Sexual abuse of a child.*

(a) *Cases involving sexual contact.* Dishonorable discharge, forfeiture of all pay and allowances, and confinement for 20 years.

47

(b) *Other cases.* Dishonorable discharge, forfeiture of all pay and allowances, and confinement for 15 years."

(c) Paragraph 45c, Article 120c, Other sexual misconduct, is amended by inserting the following new subparagraph e:

"e. *Maximum punishment.*

(1) *Indecent viewing.* Dishonorable discharge, forfeiture of all pay and allowances, and confinement for 1 year.

(2) *Indecent visual recording.* Dishonorable discharge, forfeiture of all pay and allowances, and confinement for 5 years.

(3) *Broadcasting or distribution of an indecent visual recording.* Dishonorable discharge, forfeiture of all pay and allowances, and confinement for 7 years.

(4) *Forcible pandering.* Dishonorable discharge, forfeiture of all pay and allowances, and confinement for 12 years.

(5) *Indecent exposure.* Dishonorable discharge, forfeiture of all pay and allowances, and confinement for 1 year."

Changes to the Discussion accompanying the Manual for Courts Martial. United States

(a) A new Discussion is added following Mil. R. Evid. 101(c):

"DISCUSSION

Discussion was added to these Rules in 2013. The Discussion itself does not have the force of law, even though it may describe legal requirements derived from other sources. It is in the nature of treatise, and may be used as secondary authority. If a matter is included in a rule, it is intended that the matter be binding, unless it is clearly expressed as precatory. The Discussion will be revised from time to time as warranted by changes in applicable law. *See* Composition of the Manual for Courts-Martial in Appendix 21.

Practitioners should also refer to the Analysis of the Military Rules of Evidence contained in Appendix 22 of this Manual. The Analysis is similar to Committee Notes accompanying the Federal Rules of Evidence and is intended to address the basis of the rule, deviation from the Federal Rules of Evidence, relevant precedent, and drafters' intent."

(b) A new Discussion is added following Mil. R. Evid. 301(c):

"DISCUSSION

A military judge is not required to provide Article 31 warnings. If a witness who seems uninformed of the privileges under this rule appears likely to incriminate himself or herself, the military judge may advise the witness of the right to decline to make any answer that might tend to incriminate the witness and that any self-incriminating answer the witness might make can later be used as evidence against the witness. Counsel for any party or for the witness may ask the military judge to so advise a witness if such a request is made out of the hearing of the witness and the members, if present. Failure to so advise a witness does not make the testimony of the witness inadmissible."

(c) A new Discussion is added following Mil. R. Evid. 312(b)(2)(F):

"DISCUSSION

An examination of the unclothed body under this rule should be conducted whenever practicable by a person of the same sex as that of the person being examined; however, failure to comply with this requirement does not make an examination an unlawful search within the meaning of Mil. R. Evid. 311."

(d) A new Discussion is added following Mil. R. Evid. 312(e):

"DISCUSSION

Compelling a person to ingest substances for the purposes of locating the property described above or to compel the bodily elimination of such property is a search within the meaning of this section."

(e) A new Discussion is added following Mil. R. Evid. 312(f):

"DISCUSSION

Nothing in this rule will be deemed to interfere with the lawful authority of the armed forces to take whatever action may be necessary to preserve the health of a servicemember."

(f) A new Discussion is added following Mil. R. Evid. 314(c):

"DISCUSSION

Searches under subdivision (c) may not be conducted at a time or in a manner contrary to an express provision of a treaty or agreement to which the United States is a party; however, failure to comply with a treaty or agreement does not render a search unlawful within the meaning of Mil. R. Evid. 311."

49

(g) A new Discussion is added following Mil. R. Evid. 314(e)(2):

"**DISCUSSION**

Where a co-occupant of property is physically present at the time of the requested search and expressly states his refusal to consent to the search, a warrantless search is unreasonable as to that co-occupant and evidence from the search is inadmissible as to that co-occupant. *Georgia v. Randolph*, 547 U.S. 103 (2006)."

(h) A new Discussion is added following Mil. R. Evid. 314(f)(2):

"**DISCUSSION**

Subdivision (f)(2) requires that the official making the stop have a reasonable suspicion based on specific and articulable facts that the person being frisked is armed and dangerous. Officer safety is a factor, and the officer need not be absolutely certain that the individual detained is armed for the purposes of frisking or patting down that person's outer clothing for weapons. The test is whether a reasonably prudent person in similar circumstances would be warranted in a belief that his or her safety was in danger. The purpose of a frisk is to search for weapons or other dangerous items, including but not limited to: firearms, knives, needles, or razor blades. A limited search of outer clothing for weapons serves to protect both the officer and the public; therefore, a frisk is reasonable under the Fourth Amendment."

(i) A new Discussion is added following Mil. R. Evid. 314(f)(3):

"**DISCUSSION**

The scope of the search is similar to the "stop and frisk" defined in subdivision (f)(2) of this rule. During the search for weapons, the official may seize any item that is immediately apparent as contraband or as evidence related to the offense serving as the basis for the stop. As a matter of safety, the official may, after conducting a lawful stop of a vehicle, order the driver and any passengers out of the car without any additional suspicion or justification."

(j) A new Discussion is added following Mil. R. Evid. 314(g)(2):

"**DISCUSSION**

The scope of the search for weapons is limited to that which is necessary to protect the arresting official. The official may not search a vehicle for weapons if there is no possibility that the arrestee could reach into the searched area, for example, after the arrestee is handcuffed and removed from the vehicle. The scope of the search is broader for destructible evidence related to the offense for which the individual is being arrested. Unlike a search for weapons, the search for destructible offense-related evidence may take place after the arrestee is handcuffed and removed from a vehicle. If, however, the official cannot expect to find destructible offense-related evidence, this exception does not apply."

(k) A new Discussion is added following Mil. R. Evid. 315(a):

"**DISCUSSION**

Although military personnel should adhere to procedural guidance regarding the conduct of searches, violation of such procedural guidance does not render evidence inadmissible unless the search is unlawful under these rules or the Constitution of the United States as applied to members of the armed forces. For example, if the person whose property is to be searched is present during a search conducted pursuant to a search authorization granted under this rule, the person conducting the search should notify him or her of the fact of authorization and the general substance of the authorization. Such notice may be made prior to or contemporaneously with the search. Property seized should be inventoried at the time of a seizure or as soon thereafter as practicable. A copy of the inventory should be given to a person from whose possession or premises the property was taken. Failure to provide notice, make an inventory, furnish a copy thereof, or otherwise comply with this guidance does not render a search or seizure unlawful within the meaning of Mil. R. Evid. 311."

50

(l) A new Discussion is added following Mil. R. Evid. 315(c)(4):

"DISCUSSION

If nonmilitary property within a foreign country is owned, used, occupied by, or in the possession of an agency of the United States other than the Department of Defense, a search should be conducted in coordination with an appropriate representative of the agency concerned, although failure to obtain such coordination would not render a search unlawful within the meaning of Mil. R. Evid. 311. If other nonmilitary property within a foreign country is to be searched, the search should be conducted in accordance with any relevant treaty or agreement or in coordination with an appropriate representative of the foreign country, although failure to obtain such coordination or noncompliance with a treaty or agreement would not render a search unlawful within the meaning of Mil. R. Evid. 311."

(m) A new Discussion is added following Mil. R. Evid. 317(b):

"DISCUSSION

Pursuant to 18 U.S.C. § 2516(1), the Attorney General, Deputy Attorney General, Associate Attorney General, or any Assistant Attorney General, any acting Assistant Attorney General, or any Deputy Assistant Attorney General or acting Deputy Assistant Attorney General in the Criminal Division or National Security Division specially designated by the Attorney General, may authorize an application to a Federal judge of competent jurisdiction for, and such judge may grant in conformity with 18 U.S.C. §2518, an order authorizing or approving the interception of wire or oral communications by the Federal Bureau of Investigation, or a Federal agency having responsibility for the investigation of the offense as to which the application is made, for purposes of obtaining evidence concerning the offenses enumerated in 18 U.S.C. §2516(1), to the extent such offenses are punishable under the Uniform Code of Military Justice."

(n) A new Discussion is added following Mil. R. Evid. 505(k)(3):

"DISCUSSION

In addition to the Sixth Amendment right of an accused to a public trial, the Supreme Court has held that the press and general public have a constitutional right under the First Amendment to access to criminal trials. *United States v. Hershey*, 20 M.J. 433, 436 (C.M.A. 1985) (citing *Richmond Newspapers, Inc. v. Virginia*, 448 U.S. 555 (1980)). The test that must be met before closure of a criminal trial to the public is set out in *Press-Enterprise Co. v. Superior Court*, 464 U.S. 501 (1984), to wit: the presumption of openness "may be overcome by an overriding interest based on findings that closure is essential to preserve higher values and is narrowly tailored to serve that interest. The military judge must consider reasonable alternatives to closure and must make adequate findings supporting the closure to aid in review."

51

[FR Doc. 2013–12157

Filed 5–20–13; 8:45 am]

Billing code 5001–06–C

2014 Amendments

Presidential Documents

Executive Order 13669 of June 13, 2014

2014 Amendments to the Manual for Courts-Martial, United States

By the authority vested in me as President by the Constitution and the laws of the United States of America, including chapter 47 of title 10, United States Code (Uniform Code of Military Justice, 10 U.S.C. 801–946), and in order to prescribe amendments to the Manual for Courts-Martial, United States, prescribed by Executive Order 12473 of April 13, 1984, as amended, it is hereby ordered as follows:

Section 1. Part II, the Discussion for Part II, and the Analysis for Part II of the Manual for Courts-Martial, United States, are amended as described in the Annex attached and made a part of this order.

Sec. 2. These amendments shall take effect as of the date of this order, subject to the following:

(a) Nothing in these amendments shall be construed to make punishable any act done or omitted prior to the effective date of this order that was not punishable when done or omitted.

(b) Nothing in these amendments shall be construed to invalidate any non-judicial punishment proceedings, restraint, investigation, referral of charges, trial in which arraignment occurred, or other action begun prior to the effective date of this order, and any such nonjudicial punishment, restraint, investigation, referral of charges, trial, or other action may proceed in the same manner and with the same effect as if these amendments had not been prescribed.

THE WHITE HOUSE,
June 13, 2014.

Billing code 3295–F4–P

ANNEX

Section 1. Part II of the Manual for Courts-Martial, United States, is amended as follows:

(a) R.C.M. 405(f)(10) is amended to read as follows:

"(10) Have evidence, including documents or physical evidence, produced as provided under subsection (g) of this rule;".

(b) R.C.M. 405(g)(1)(B) is amended to read as follows:

"(B) *Evidence*. Subject to Mil. R. Evid., Section V, evidence, including documents or physical evidence, which is relevant to the investigation and not cumulative, shall be produced if reasonably available. Such evidence includes evidence requested by the accused, if the request is timely and in compliance with this rule. As soon as practicable after receipt of a request by the accused for information that may be protected under Mil. R. Evid. 505 or 506, the investigating officer shall notify the person who is authorized to issue a protective order under subsection (g)(6) of this rule, and the convening authority, if different. Evidence is reasonably available if its significance outweighs the difficulty, expense, delay, and effect on military operations of obtaining the evidence."

(c) R.C.M. 405(g)(2)(C) is amended to read as follows:

"(C) *Evidence generally*. The investigating officer shall make an initial determination whether evidence is reasonably available. If the investigating officer decides that it is not reasonably available, the investigating officer shall inform the parties."

(d) R.C.M. 405(g)(2)(C)(i) is inserted to read as follows:

"(i) *Evidence under the control of the Government.* Upon the investigating officer's determination that evidence is reasonably available, the custodian of the evidence shall be requested to provide the evidence. A determination by the custodian that the evidence is not reasonably available is not subject to appeal by the accused, but may be reviewed by the military judge under R.C.M. 906(b)(3)."

(e) R.C.M. 405(g)(2)(C)(ii) is inserted to read as follows:

"(ii) *Evidence not under the control of the Government.* Evidence not under the control of the Government may be obtained through noncompulsory means or by subpoena duces tecum issued pursuant to procedures set forth in R.C.M. 703(f)(4)(B). A determination by the investigating officer that the evidence is not reasonably available is not subject to appeal by the accused, but may be reviewed by the military judge under R.C.M. 906(b)(3)."

(f) R.C.M. 405(i) is amended to read as follows:

"(i) *Military Rules of Evidence.* The Military Rules of Evidence do not apply in pretrial investigations under this rule except as follows:

2

(1) Military Rules of Evidence 301, 302, 303, 305, and Section V shall apply in their entirety.

(2) Military Rule of Evidence 412 shall apply in any case defined as a sexual offense in Mil. R. Evid. 412(d).

(3) In applying these rules to a pretrial investigation, the term "military judge," as used in these rules, shall mean the investigating officer, who shall assume the military judge's powers to exclude evidence from the pretrial investigation, and who shall, in discharging this duty, follow the procedures set forth in the rules cited in paragraphs (1) and (2)."

(g) R.C.M. 703(e)(2)(B) is amended to read as follows:

"(B) *Contents.* A subpoena shall state the command by which the proceeding is directed, and the title, if any, of the proceeding. A subpoena shall command each person to whom it is directed to attend and give testimony at the time and place specified therein. A subpoena may also command the person to whom it is directed to produce books, papers, documents, data, or other objects or electronically stored information designated therein at the proceeding or at an earlier time for inspection by the parties. A subpoena issued for an investigation pursuant to Article 32 shall not command any person to attend or give testimony at an Article 32 investigation."

(h) R.C.M. 703(e)(2)(C) is amended to read as follows:

3

"(C) *Who may issue.*

(1)   A subpoena to secure evidence may be issued by:

(a) the summary court-martial;

(b) detailed counsel representing the United States at an Article 32 investigation;

(c) the investigating officer appointed under R.C.M. 405(d)(1);

(d) after referral to a court-martial, detailed trial counsel;

(e)   the president of a court of inquiry; or

(f)   an officer detailed to take a deposition.

(2)   A subpoena to secure witnesses may be issued by:

(a) the summary court-martial;

(b) after referral to a court-martial, detailed trial counsel;

(c)   the president of a court of inquiry; or

(d)   an officer detailed to take a deposition.

(i) R.C.M. 703(e)(2)(D) is amended to read as follows:

"(D) *Service.* A subpoena may be served by the person authorized by this rule to issue it, a United States Marshal, or any other person who is not less than 18 years of age. Service shall be made by delivering a copy of the subpoena to the person named and by providing to the person named travel orders and a means for reimbursement for fees and mileage as may be

4

prescribed by the Secretary concerned, or in the case of hardship resulting in the subpoenaed witness's inability to comply with the subpoena absent initial government payment, by providing to the person named travel orders, fees, and mileage sufficient to comply with the subpoena in rules prescribed by the Secretary concerned."

(j) R.C.M. 703(e)(2)(G)(ii) is amended to read as follows:

"(ii) *Requirements.* A warrant of attachment may be issued only upon probable cause to believe that the witness was duly served with a subpoena, that the subpoena was issued in accordance with these rules, that a means of reimbursement of fees and mileage was provided to the witness or advanced to the witness in cases of hardship, that the witness is material, that the witness refused or willfully neglected to appear at the time and place specified on the subpoena, and that no valid excuse is reasonably apparent for the witness's failure to appear."

(k) R.C.M. 703(f)(4)(B) is amended to read as follows:

"(B) *Evidence not under the control of the Government.* Evidence not under the control of the Government may be obtained by subpoena issued in accordance with subsection (e)(2) of this rule. A subpoena duces tecum to produce books, papers, documents, data, or other objects or electronically stored information for a pretrial investigation pursuant to Article 32 may be issued, following the convening authority's order

5

directing such pretrial investigation, by either the investigating officer appointed under R.C.M. 405(d)(1) or the detailed counsel representing the United States. A person in receipt of a subpoena duces tecum for an Article 32 hearing need not personally appear in order to comply with the subpoena."

(1) R.C.M. 1103(b)(3) is amended by inserting new subsection (N) after R.C.M. 1103(b)(3)(M) as follows:

"(N) Documents pertaining to the receipt of the record of trial by the victim pursuant to subsection (g)(3) of this rule."

(m) R.C.M. 1103(g) is amended by inserting new subsection (3) after R.C.M. 1103(g)(2) as follows:

"(3) *Cases involving sexual offenses.*

(A) "Victim" defined. For the purposes of this rule, a victim is a person who suffered a direct physical, emotional, or pecuniary harm as a result of matters set forth in a charge or specification; and is named in a specification under Article 120, Article 120b, Article 120c, Article 125, or any attempt to commit such offense in violation of Article 80.

(B) *Scope; qualifying victim.* In a general or special court-martial, a copy of the record of trial shall be given free of charge to a victim as defined in subparagraph (A) for a specification identified in subparagraph (A) that resulted in any finding under R.C.M. 918(a)(1). If a victim is a minor, a

6

copy of the record of trial shall instead be provided to the parent or legal guardian of the victim.

(C) *Notice.* In accordance with regulations of the Secretary concerned, and no later than authentication of the record, trial counsel shall cause each qualifying victim to be notified of the opportunity to receive a copy of the record of trial. Qualifying victims may decline receipt of such documents in writing and any written declination shall be attached to the original record of trial.

(D) *Documents to be provided.* For purposes of this subsection, the record of trial shall consist of documents described in subsection (b)(2) of this rule, except for proceedings described in subsection (e) of this rule, in which case the record of trial shall consist of items described in subsection (e). Matters attached to the record as described in subsection (b)(3) of this rule are not required to be provided."

(n) R.C.M. 1104(b)(1) is amended by inserting new subsection (E) after the Discussion section to R.C.M. 1104(b)(1)(D)(iii)(d) as follows:

"(E) *Victims of Sexual Assault.* Qualifying victims, as defined in R.C.M. 1103(g)(3)(A), shall be served a copy of the record of trial in the same manner as the accused under subsection (b) of this rule. In accordance with regulations of the Secretary concerned:

7

(i) A copy of the record of trial shall be provided to each qualifying victim as soon as it is authenticated or, if the victim requests, at a time thereafter. The victim's receipt of the record of trial, including any delay in receiving it, shall be documented and attached to the original record of trial.

(ii) A copy of the convening authority's action as described in R.C.M. 1103(b)(2)(D)(iv) shall be provided to each qualifying victim as soon as each document is prepared. If the victim makes a request in writing, service of the record of trial may be delayed until the action is available.

(iii) Classified information pursuant to subsection (b)(1)(D) of this rule, sealed matters pursuant to R.C.M. 1103A, or other portions of the record the release of which would unlawfully violate the privacy interests of any party, to include those afforded by 5 U.S.C. § 552a, the Privacy Act of 1974, shall not be provided. Matters attached to the record as described in R.C.M. 1103(b)(3) are not required to be provided."

(o) R.C.M. 1105A is newly inserted and reads as follows:

"Rule 1105A. Matters submitted by a crime victim

(a) *In general.* A crime victim of an offense tried by any court-martial shall have the right to submit a written statement to the convening authority after the sentence is adjudged.

8

(b) *"Crime victim" defined.* For purposes of this rule, a crime victim is a person who has suffered direct physical, emotional, or pecuniary harm as a result of the commission of an offense of which the accused was found guilty, and on which the convening authority is taking action under R.C.M. 1107. When a victim is under 18 years of age, incompetent, incapacitated, or deceased, the term includes one of the following (in order of precedence): a spouse, legal guardian, parent, child, sibling, or similarly situated family member. For a victim that is an institutional entity, the term includes an authorized representative of the entity.

(c) *Format of statement.* The statement shall be in writing, and signed by the crime victim. Statements may include photographs, but shall not include video, audio, or other media.

(d) *Timing of statement.*

(1) *General and special courts-martial.* The crime victim shall submit the statement to the convening authority's staff judge advocate or legal officer no later than 10 days after the later of:

(A) if the victim is entitled to a copy of the record of proceedings in accordance with Article 54(e), UCMJ, the date on which the victim receives an authenticated copy of the record of trial or waives the right to receive such a copy; or

9

(B) the date on which the recommendation of the staff judge advocate or legal officer is served on the victim.

(2) *Summary courts-martial*. The crime victim shall submit the statement to the summary court-martial officer no later than 7 days after the sentence is announced.

(3) Extensions. If a victim shows that additional time is required for submission of matters, the convening authority or other person taking action, for good cause, may extend the submission period for not more than an additional 20 days.

(e) *Notice*. Subject to such regulations as the Secretary concerned may prescribe, trial counsel or the summary court-martial officer shall make reasonable efforts to inform crime victims of their rights under this rule, and shall advise such crime victims on the manner in which their statements may be submitted.

(f) *Waiver*.

(1) *Failure to submit a statement*. Failure to submit a statement within the time prescribed by this rule shall be deemed a waiver of the right to submit such a statement.

(2) *Submission of a statement*. Submission of a statement under this rule shall be deemed a waiver of the right to submit an additional statement.

10

(3) *Written waiver.* A crime victim may expressly waive, in writing, the right to submit a statement under this rule. Once filed, such waiver may not be revoked."

(p) R.C.M. 1106(a) is amended to read as follows:

"(a) *In general.* Before the convening authority takes action under R.C.M. 1107 on a record of trial by general court-martial, on a record of trial by special court-martial that includes a sentence to a bad-conduct discharge or confinement for one year, or on a record of trial by special court-martial in which a victim is entitled to submit a statement pursuant to R.C.M. 1105A, that convening authority's staff judge advocate or legal officer shall, except as provided in subsection (c) of this rule, forward to the convening authority a recommendation under this rule."

(q) R.C.M. 1106(d)(3) is amended to read as follows:

"(3) *Required contents.* Except as provided in subsection (e), the staff judge advocate or legal advisor shall provide the convening authority with a copy of the report of results of the trial, setting forth the findings, sentence, and confinement credit to be applied; a copy or summary of the pretrial agreement, if any; a copy of any statement submitted by a crime victim pursuant to R.C.M. 1105A; any recommendation for clemency by the sentencing authority made in conjunction with the

11

announced sentence; and the staff judge advocate's concise recommendation."

(r) R.C.M. 1106(f) and (f)(1) are amended to read as follows:

"(f) *Service of recommendation on defense counsel, accused, and victim; defense response.*

(1) *Service of recommendation on defense counsel, accused, and victim.* Before forwarding the recommendation and the record of trial to the convening authority for action under R.C.M. 1107, the staff judge advocate or legal officer shall cause a copy of the recommendation to be served on the counsel for the accused. A separate copy will be served on the accused. If it is impracticable to serve the recommendation on the accused for reasons including the transfer of the accused to a different place, the unauthorized absence of the accused, or military exigency, or if the accused so requests on the record at the court-martial or in writing, the accused's copy shall be forwarded to the accused's defense counsel. A statement shall be attached to the record explaining why the accused was not served personally. If the accused was found guilty of any offense that resulted in direct physical, emotional, or pecuniary harm to a victim or victims, a separate copy of the recommendation will be served on that victim or those victims. When a victim is under 18 years of age, incompetent, incapacitated, deceased, or otherwise unavailable, service shall be made on one of the

12

following (in order of precedence): the victim's attorney, spouse, legal guardian, parent, child, sibling, or similarly situated family member. For a victim that is an institutional entity, service shall be made on an authorized representative of the entity.

(s) R.C.M. 1106(f)(4) is amended to read as follows:

"(4) *Response.* Counsel for the accused may submit, in writing, corrections or rebuttal to any matter in the recommendation and its enclosures believed to be erroneous, inadequate, or misleading, and may comment on any other matter."

(t) R.C.M. 1107(b)(3)(A) is amended by inserting new subsection (iv) immediately after R.C.M. 1107(b)(3)(A)(iii) as follows:

"(iv) Any statement submitted by a crime victim pursuant to R.C.M. 1105A."

(u) R.C.M. 1107(b)(3) is amended by inserting new subsection (C) immediately after R.C.M. 1107(b)(3)(B)(iii) as follows:

"(C) *Prohibited matters.* The convening authority shall not consider any matters that relate to the character of a victim unless such matters were presented as evidence at trial and not excluded at trial."

(v) R.C.M. 1306(a) is amended to read as follows:

"(a) *Matters submitted.*

(1) *By a crime victim.* After a sentence is adjudged, a crime victim may submit a written statement to the convening

13

authority in accordance with R.C.M. 1105A. A statement submitted by a crime victim shall be immediately served on the accused.

(2) *By the accused*. After a sentence is adjudged, the accused may submit written matters to the convening authority in accordance with R.C.M. 1105."

Sec. 2. The Discussion to Part II of the Manual for Courts-Martial, United States, is amended as follows:

(a) The Discussion immediately following R.C.M. 306(b) is amended to read as follows:

"The disposition decision is one of the most important and difficult decisions facing a commander. Many factors must be taken into consideration and balanced, including, to the extent practicable, the nature of the offenses, any mitigating or extenuating circumstances, the views of the victim as to disposition, any recommendations made by subordinate commanders, the interest of justice, military exigencies, and the effect of the decision on the accused and the command. The goal should be a disposition that is warranted, appropriate, and fair.

In deciding how an offense should be disposed of, factors the commander should consider, to the extent they are known, include:

(A) the nature of and circumstances surrounding the offense and the extent of the harm caused by the offense, including the

14

offense's effect on morale, health, safety, welfare, and discipline;

(B) when applicable, the views of the victim as to disposition;

(C) existence of jurisdiction over the accused and the offense;

(D) availability and admissibility of evidence;

(E) the willingness of the victim or others to testify;

(F) cooperation of the accused in the apprehension or prosecution of another accused;

(G) possible improper motives or biases of the person(s) making the allegation(s);

(H) availability and likelihood of prosecution of the same or similar and related charges against the accused by another jurisdiction;

(I) appropriateness of the authorized punishment to the particular accused or offense.

(b) The Discussion immediately following R.C.M. 405(g)(1)(B) is amended to read as follows:

"In preparing for the investigation, the investigating officer should consider what evidence, including evidence that may be obtained by subpoena duces tecum, will be necessary to prepare a thorough and impartial investigation. The investigating officer should consider, as to potential witnesses, whether their

15

personal appearance will be necessary. Generally, personal appearance is preferred, but the investigating officer should consider whether, in light of the probable importance of a witness's testimony, an alternative to testimony under subsection (g)(4)(A) of this rule would be sufficient.

After making a preliminary determination of what witnesses will be produced and other evidence considered, the investigating officer should notify the defense and inquire whether it requests the production of other witnesses or evidence. In addition to witnesses for the defense, the defense may request production of witnesses whose testimony would favor the prosecution.

Once it is determined what witnesses the investigating officer intends to call, it must be determined whether each witness is reasonably available. That determination is a balancing test. The more important the testimony of the witness, the greater the difficulty, expense, delay, or effect on military operations must be to permit nonproduction. For example, the temporary absence of a witness on leave for 10 days would normally justify using an alternative to that witness's personal appearance if the sole reason for the witness's testimony was to impeach the credibility of another witness by reputation evidence, or to establish a mitigating character trait of the accused. On the other hand, if the same witness was the only eyewitness to the

16

offense, personal appearance would be required if the defense requested it and the witness is otherwise reasonably available. The time and place of the investigation may be changed if reasonably necessary to permit the appearance of a witness. Similar considerations apply to the production of evidence, including evidence that may be obtained by subpoena duces tecum.

If the production of witnesses or evidence would entail substantial costs or delay, the investigating officer should inform the commander who directed the investigation.

The provision in (B), requiring the investigating officer to notify the appropriate authorities of requests by the accused for information privileged under Mil. R. Evid. 505 or 506, is for the purpose of placing the appropriate authority on notice that an order, as authorized under subsection (g)(6), may be required to protect whatever information the government may decide to release to the accused."

(c) The Discussion immediately following R.C.M. 405(g)(2)(B) is amended to read as follows:

"The investigating officer should initially determine whether a civilian witness is reasonably available without regard to whether the witness is willing to appear. If the investigating officer determines that a civilian witness is apparently reasonably available, the witness should be invited to attend

17

and, when appropriate, informed that necessary expenses will be paid.

If the witness refuses to testify, the witness is not reasonably available because civilian witnesses may not be compelled to attend a pretrial investigation. Under subsection (g)(3) of this rule, civilian witnesses may be paid for travel and associated expenses to testify at a pretrial investigation. Except for use in support of the deposition of a witness under Article 49, UCMJ, and ordered pursuant to R.C.M. 702(b), the investigating officer and any government representative to an Article 32, UCMJ, proceeding does not possess authority to issue a subpoena to compel against his or her will a civilian witness to appear and provide testimony."

(d) The Discussion immediately following R.C.M. 405(g)(2)(C)(i) is amended to read as follows:

"Evidence shall include documents and physical evidence that are relevant to the investigation and not cumulative. *See* subsection (g)(1)(B). The investigating officer may discuss factors affecting reasonable availability with the custodian and with others. If the custodian determines that the evidence is not reasonably available, the reasons for that determination should be provided to the investigating officer."

(e) The following Discussion is inserted immediately after R.C.M. 405(g)(2)(C)(ii):

18

"A subpoena duces tecum to produce books, papers, documents, data, electronically stored information, or other objects for a pretrial investigation pursuant to Article 32 may be issued by the investigating officer or counsel representing the United States. *See* R.C.M. 703(f)(4)(B).

The investigating officer may find that evidence is not reasonably available if: the subpoenaed party refuses to comply with the duly issued subpoena duces tecum; the evidence is not subject to compulsory process; or the significance of the evidence is outweighed by the difficulty, expense, delay, and effect on military operations of obtaining the evidence."

(f) The Discussion immediately following R.C.M. 405(g)(3) is amended to read as follows:

"*See* Department of Defense Joint Travel Regulations, Vol. 2, paragraph C7055."

(g) The Discussion immediately following R.C.M. 405(i) is amended to read as follows:

"With regard to all evidence, the investigating officer should exercise reasonable control over the scope of the inquiry. *See* subsection (e) of this rule. An investigating officer may consider any evidence, even if that evidence would not be admissible at trial. However, see subsection (g)(4) of this rule as to limitations on the ways in which testimony may be presented. Certain rules relating to the form of testimony that

19

may be considered by the investigating officer appear in subsection (g) of this rule.

Mil. R. Evid. 412 evidence, including closed hearing testimony, must be protected pursuant to the Privacy Act of 1974, 5 U.S.C. § 552a. Evidence deemed admissible by the investigating officer should be made a part of the report of investigation. *See* subsection (j)(2)(C), *infra*. Evidence deemed inadmissible, and the testimony taken during the closed hearing, should not be included in the report of investigation and should be safeguarded. The investigating officer and counsel representing the United States are responsible for careful handling of any such evidence to prevent indiscriminate viewing or disclosure. Although R.C.M. 1103A does not apply, its requirements should be used as a model for safeguarding inadmissible evidence and closed hearing testimony. The convening authority and the appropriate judge advocate are permitted to review such safeguarded evidence and testimony. *See* R.C.M. 601(d)(1)."

(h) The Discussion immediately following R.C.M. 703(e)(2)(B) is amended to read as follows:

"A subpoena may not be used to compel a witness to appear at an examination or interview before trial, but a subpoena may be used to obtain witnesses for a deposition or a court of inquiry. In accordance with subsection (f)(4)(B) of this rule, a subpoena

20

duces tecum to produce books, papers, documents, data, or other objects or electronically stored information for pretrial investigation pursuant to Article 32 may be issued, following the convening authority's order directing such pretrial investigation, by either the investigating officer appointed under R.C.M. 405(d)(1) or the counsel representing the United States.

A subpoena normally is prepared, signed, and issued in duplicate on the official forms. *See* Appendix 7 for an example of a subpoena with certificate of service (DD Form 453) and a Travel Order (DD Form 453-1)."

(i) The Discussion immediately following R.C.M. 703(e)(2)(D) is amended to read as follows:

"If practicable, a subpoena should be issued in time to permit service at least 24 hours before the time the witness will have to travel to comply with the subpoena.

Informal service. Unless formal service is advisable, the person who issued the subpoena may mail it to the witness in duplicate, enclosing a postage-paid envelope bearing a return address, with the request that the witness sign the acceptance of service on the copy and return it in the envelope provided. The return envelope should be addressed to the person who issued the subpoena. The person who issued the subpoena should include with it a statement to the effect that the rights of the witness

21

to fees and mileage will not be impaired by voluntary compliance with the request and that a voucher for fees and mileage will be delivered to the witness promptly on being discharged from attendance.

Formal service. Formal service is advisable whenever it is anticipated that the witness will not comply voluntarily with the subpoena. Appropriate fees and mileage must be paid or tendered. *See* Article 47. If formal service is advisable, the person who issued the subpoena must assure timely and economical service. That person may do so by serving the subpoena personally when the witness is in the vicinity. When the witness is not in the vicinity, the subpoena may be sent in duplicate to the commander of a military installation near the witness. Such commanders should give prompt and effective assistance, issuing travel orders for their personnel to serve the subpoena when necessary.

Service should ordinarily be made by a person subject to the code. The duplicate copy of the subpoena must have entered upon it proof of service as indicated on the form and must be promptly returned to the person who issued the subpoena. If service cannot be made, the person who issued the subpoena must be informed promptly. A stamped, addressed envelope should be provided for these purposes.

22

For purposes of this Rule, *hardship* is defined as any situation which would substantially preclude reasonable efforts to appear that could be solved by providing transportation or fees and mileage to which the witness is entitled for appearing at the hearing in question."

(j) The Discussion immediately following R.C.M. 703(e)(2)(G)(i) is amended to read as follows:

"A warrant of attachment (DD Form 454) may be used when necessary to compel a witness to appear or produce evidence under this rule. A warrant of attachment is a legal order addressed to an official directing that official to have the person named in the order brought before a court.

Subpoenas issued under R.C.M. 703 are Federal process and a person not subject to the code may be prosecuted in a Federal civilian court under Article 47 for failure to comply with a subpoena issued in compliance with this rule and formally served.

Failing to comply with such a subpoena is a felony offense, and may result in a fine or imprisonment, or both, at the discretion of the district court. The different purposes of the warrant of attachment and criminal complaint under Article 47 should be borne in mind. The warrant of attachment, available without the intervention of civilian judicial proceedings, has as its purpose the obtaining of the witness's presence,

23

testimony, or documents. The criminal complaint, prosecuted through the civilian Federal courts, has as its purpose punishment for failing to comply with process issued by military authority. It serves to vindicate the military interest in obtaining compliance with its lawful process.

For subpoenas issued for a pretrial investigation pursuant to Article 32 under subsection (f)(4)(B), the general court-martial convening authority with jurisdiction over the case may issue a warrant of attachment to compel production of documents."

(k) The Discussion immediately following R.C.M. 703(f)(1) is amended to read as follows:

"Relevance is defined by Mil. R. Evid. 401. Relevant evidence is necessary when it is not cumulative and when it would contribute to a party's presentation of the case in some positive way on a matter in issue. A matter is not in issue when it is stipulated as a fact. The discovery and introduction of classified or other government information is controlled by Mil. R. Evid. 505 and 506."

(l) The following Discussion is added immediately after R.C.M. 703(f)(4)(B):

"The National Defense Authorization Act for Fiscal Year 2012, P.L. 112-81, § 542, amended Article 47 to allow the issuance of subpoenas duces tecum for Article 32 hearings. Although the amended language cites Article 32(b), this new subpoena power

24

extends to documents subpoenaed by the investigating officer and counsel representing the United States, whether or not requested by the defense."

(m) The following Discussion is inserted immediately after R.C.M. 1103(b)(3)(N):

"Per R.C.M. 1114(f), consult service regulations for distribution of promulgating orders."

(n) The following Discussion is added immediately after R.C.M. 1103(g)(3)(B):

"This rule is not intended to limit the Services' discretion to provide records of trial to other individuals."

(o) The following Discussion is inserted immediately after R.C.M. 1103(g)(3)(D):

"Subsections (b)(3)(N) and (g)(3) of this rule were added to implement Article 54(e), UCMJ, in compliance with the National Defense Authorization Act for Fiscal Year 2012 (P.L. 112-81, § 586). Service of a copy of the record of trial on a victim is prescribed in R.C.M. 1104(b)(1)(E)."

(p) The following Discussion is added immediately after R.C.M. 1104(b)(1)(E):

"Subsection (b)(1)(E) of this rule was added to implement Article 54(e), UCMJ, in compliance with the National Defense Authorization Act for Fiscal Year 2012 (P.L. 112-81, § 586). The

25

content of the victim's record of trial is prescribed in R.C.M. 1103(g)(3)(D).

Promulgating orders are to be distributed in accordance with R.C.M. 1114(f)."

(q) The following Discussion is added immediately after R.C.M. 1105A(c):

"Statements should be submitted to the convening authority's staff judge advocate or legal officer, or, in the case of a summary court-martial, to the summary court-martial officer."

(r) The Discussion immediately after R.C.M. 1106(d)(3) is amended to read as follows:

"The recommendation required by this rule need not include information regarding the recommendations for clemency. *See* R.C.M. 1105(b)(2)(D), which pertains to clemency recommendations that may be submitted by the accused to the convening authority.

The recommendation is only required to include a crime victim's statement if the statement is submitted by the crime victim under the provisions of R.C.M. 1105A. The recommendation is not required to contain any other statements that a crime victim may have made on other occasions unless those previous statements are submitted by the crime victim under the provisions of R.C.M. 1105A."

(s) The Discussion immediately after R.C.M. 1106(f)(7) is amended to read as follows:

26

""New matter" includes discussion of the effect of new decisions on issues in the case, matter from outside the record of trial, and issues not previously discussed. "New matter" does not ordinarily include any discussion by the staff judge advocate or legal officer of the correctness of the initial defense comments on the recommendation. The method of service and the form of the proof of service are not prescribed and may be by any appropriate means. *See* R.C.M. 1103(b)(3)(G). For example, a certificate of service, attached to the record of trial, would be appropriate when the accused is served personally. If a victim statement, submitted under R.C.M. 1105A, is served on the accused prior to service of the recommendation, then that statement shall not be considered a "new matter" when it is again served on the accused as an enclosure to the recommendation."

Sec. 3. Appendix 21 of the Manual for Courts-Martial, United States, Analysis of Rules for Courts-Martial, is amended as follows:

R.C.M. 1107, after the paragraph beginning with the words "Subsection (3)(A)(i)," insert the following language:

"*2014 Amendment.* The prohibition against considering matters that relate to the character of a victim expands upon the prohibition against considering "submitted" matters that is

27

set forth in section 1706(b) of the National Defense

Authorization Act for Fiscal Year 2014, Pub. L. No. 113-66, 127

Stat. 961 (2013). This revision does not incorporate the word

"submitted" from section 1706(b), in order to afford greater

protection to the victim by prohibiting convening authority

consideration of any evidence of a victim's character not

admitted into evidence at trial, no matter the source."

28

[FR Doc. 2014–14429

Filed 6–17–14; 11:15 a.m.]

Billing code 5001–06–C

2015 Amendments

Presidential Documents

Title 3—

The President

Executive Order 13696 of June 17, 2015

2015 Amendments to the Manual for Courts-Martial, United States

By the authority vested in me as President by the Constitution and the laws of the United States of America, including chapter 47 of title 10, United States Code (Uniform Code of Military Justice, 10 U.S.C. 801–946), and in order to prescribe amendments to the Manual for Courts-Martial, United States, prescribed by Executive Order 12473 of April 13, 1984, as amended, it is hereby ordered as follows:

Section 1. Part II, Part III, and Part IV of the Manual for Courts-Martial, United States, are amended as described in the Annex attached and made a part of this order.

Sec. 2. These amendments shall take effect as of the date of this order, subject to the following:

(a) Nothing in these amendments shall be construed to make punishable any act done or omitted prior to the effective date of this order that was not punishable when done or omitted.

(b) Nothing in these amendments shall be construed to invalidate any nonjudicial punishment proceedings, restraint, investigation, referral of charges, trial in which arraignment occurred, or other action begun prior to the effective date of this order, and any such nonjudicial punishment, restraint, investigation, referral of charges, trial, or other action may proceed in the same manner and with the same effect as if these amendments had not been prescribed.

THE WHITE HOUSE,

June 17, 2015.

Billing code 3295–F5

ANNEX

Section 1. Part II of the Manual for Courts-Martial, United States, is amended as follows:

(a) R.C.M. 201(f)(1) is amended to insert the following after "Types of courts-martial" and before "(1) General courts-martial":

"[Note: R.C.M. 201(f)(1)(D) and (f)(2)(D) apply to offenses committed on or after 24 June 2014.]"

(b) R.C.M. 201(f)(1)(D) is inserted immediately after R.C.M. 201(f)(1)(C) and reads as follows:

"(D) *Jurisdiction for Certain Sexual Offenses.* Only a general court-martial has jurisdiction to try offenses under Article 120(a), 120(b), 120b(a), and 120b(b), forcible sodomy under Article 125, and attempts thereof under Article 80."

(c) R.C.M. 201(f)(2)(D) is inserted immediately after R.C.M. 201(f)(2)(C)(iii) and reads as follows:

"(D) *Certain Offenses under Articles 120, 120b, and 125.* Notwithstanding subsection (f)(2)(A), special courts-martial do not have jurisdiction over offenses under Articles 120(a), 120(b), 120b(a), and 120b(b), forcible sodomy under Article 125, and attempts thereof under Article 80. Such offenses shall not be referred to a special court-martial."

(d) R.C.M. 305(i)(2)(A)(i) is amended to read as follows:

"(i) *Matters considered.* The review under this subsection shall include a review of the memorandum submitted by the prisoner's commander under subsection (h)(2)(C) of this rule. Additional written matters may be considered, including any submitted by the prisoner. The prisoner and the prisoner's counsel, if any, shall be allowed to appear before the 7-day reviewing officer and make a statement, if practicable. A representative of the command may also appear before the reviewing officer to make a statement."

(e) R.C.M. 305(i)(2)(A)(iv) is inserted immediately after R.C.M. 305(i)(2)(A)(iii) and reads as follows:

"(iv) *Victim's right to be reasonably heard.* A victim of an alleged offense committed by the prisoner has the right to reasonable, accurate, and timely notice of the 7-day review; the right to confer with the representative of the command and counsel for the government, if any, and the right to be reasonably heard during the review. However, the hearing may not be unduly delayed for this purpose. The right to be heard under this rule includes the right to be heard through counsel. The victim of an alleged offense shall be notified of these rights in accordance with regulations of the Secretary concerned."

(f) R.C.M. 305(i)(2)(C) is amended to read as follows:

"(C) *Action by 7-day reviewing officer.* Upon completion of review, the reviewing officer shall approve continued confinement or order immediate release. If the reviewing officer orders immediate release, a victim of an alleged offense committed by the prisoner has the right to reasonable, accurate, and timely notice of the release, unless such notice may endanger the safety of any person."

(g) R.C.M. 305(i)(2)(D) is amended to read as follows:

"(D) *Memorandum.* The 7-day reviewing officer's conclusions, including the factual findings on which they are based, shall be set forth in a written memorandum. The memorandum shall also state whether the victim was notified of the review, was given the opportunity to confer with the representative of the command or counsel for the government, and was given a reasonable opportunity to be heard. A copy of the memorandum and all documents considered by the 7-day reviewing officer shall be maintained in accordance with regulations prescribed by the Secretary concerned and provided to the accused or the Government on request."

(h) R.C.M. 305(n) is inserted immediately after R.C.M. 305(m)(2) and reads as follows:

"(n) *Notice to victim of escaped prisoner.* A victim of an alleged offense committed by the prisoner for which the prisoner has been placed in pretrial confinement has the right to reasonable, accurate, and timely notice of the escape of the prisoner, unless such notice may endanger the safety of any person."

(i) R.C.M. 404(e) is amended to read as follows:

"(e) Unless otherwise prescribed by the Secretary concerned, direct a preliminary hearing under R.C.M. 405, and, if appropriate, forward the report of preliminary hearing with the charges to a superior commander for disposition."

(j) A new rule, R.C.M. 404A, is inserted immediately after R.C.M. 404(e) and reads as follows:

"Rule 404A. Disclosure of matters following direction of preliminary hearing

(a) When a convening authority directs a preliminary hearing under R.C.M. 405, counsel for the government shall, subject to subsections (b) through (d) of this rule, within 5 days of issuance of the Article 32 appointing order, provide to the defense the following information or matters:

(1) Charge sheet;

(2) Article 32 appointing order;

(3) Documents accompanying the charge sheet on which the preferral decision was based;

(4) Documents provided to the convening authority when deciding to direct the preliminary hearing;

(5) Documents the counsel for the government intends to present at the preliminary hearing; and

(6) Access to tangible objects counsel for the government intends to present at the preliminary hearing.

(b) *Contraband*. If items covered by subsection (a) of this rule are contraband, the disclosure required under this rule is a reasonable opportunity to inspect said contraband prior to the hearing.

(c) *Privilege*. If items covered by subsection (a) of this rule are privileged, classified or otherwise protected under Section V of Part III, no disclosure of those items is required under this rule. However, counsel for the government may disclose privileged, classified, or otherwise protected information covered by subsection (a) of this rule if authorized by the holder of the privilege, or in the case of Mil. R. Evid. 505 or 506, if authorized by a competent authority.

(d) *Protective order if privileged information is disclosed*. If the government agrees to disclose to the accused information to which the protections afforded by Section V of Part III may apply, the convening authority, or other person designated by regulation of the Secretary concerned, may enter an appropriate protective order, in writing, to guard against the compromise of information disclosed to the accused. The terms of any such protective order may include prohibiting the disclosure of the information except as authorized by the authority issuing the protective order, as well as those terms specified by Mil. R. Evid. 505(g)(2)-(6) or 506(g)(2)-(5)."

(k) R.C.M. 405 is amended to read as follows:

"Rule 405. Preliminary hearing

(a) *In general*. Except as provided in subsection (k) of this rule, no charge or specification may be referred to a general court-martial for trial until completion of a preliminary hearing in substantial compliance with this rule. A preliminary hearing conducted under this rule is not intended to serve as a means of discovery and will be limited to an examination of those issues necessary to determine whether there is probable cause to conclude that an offense or offenses have been committed and whether the accused committed it; to determine whether a court-martial would have jurisdiction over the offense(s) and the accused; to consider the form of the charge(s); and to recommend the disposition that should be made of the charge(s). Failure to comply with this rule shall have no effect on the disposition of the charge(s) if the charge(s) is not referred to a general court-martial.

(b) *Earlier preliminary hearing.* If a preliminary hearing of the subject matter of an offense has been conducted before the accused is charged with an offense, and the accused was present at the preliminary hearing and afforded the rights to counsel, cross-examination, and presentation of evidence required by this rule, no further preliminary hearing is required.

(c) *Who may direct a preliminary hearing.* Unless prohibited by regulations of the Secretary concerned, a preliminary hearing may be directed under this rule by any court-martial convening authority. That authority may also give procedural instructions not inconsistent with these rules.

(d) *Personnel.*

(1) *Preliminary hearing officer.* Whenever practicable, the convening authority directing a preliminary hearing under this rule shall detail an impartial judge advocate certified under Article 27(b), not the accuser, as a preliminary hearing officer, who shall conduct the preliminary hearing and make a report that addresses whether there is probable cause to believe that an offense or offenses have been committed and that the accused committed the offense(s); whether a court-martial would have jurisdiction over the offense(s) and the accused; the form of the charges(s); and a recommendation as to the disposition of the charge(s).

When the appointment of a judge advocate as the preliminary hearing officer is not practicable, or in exceptional circumstances in which the interest of justice warrants, the convening authority directing the preliminary hearing may detail an impartial commissioned officer, who is not the accuser, as the preliminary hearing officer. If the preliminary hearing officer is not a judge advocate, an impartial judge advocate certified under Article 27(b) shall be available to provide legal advice to the preliminary hearing officer.

When practicable, the preliminary hearing officer shall be equal or senior in grade to the military counsel detailed to represent the accused and the government at the preliminary hearing. The Secretary concerned may prescribe additional limitations on the appointment of preliminary hearing officers.

The preliminary hearing officer shall not depart from an impartial role and become an advocate for either side. The preliminary hearing officer is disqualified to act later in the same case in any other capacity.

(2) *Counsel to represent the United States.* A judge advocate, not the accuser, shall serve as counsel to represent the United States, and shall present evidence on behalf of the government relevant to the limited scope and purpose of the preliminary hearing as set forth in subsection (a) of this rule.

(3) *Defense counsel.*

(A) *Detailed counsel.* Except as provided in subsection (d)(3)(B) of this rule, military counsel certified in accordance with Article 27(b) shall be detailed to represent the accused.

(B) *Individual military counsel.* The accused may request to be represented by individual military counsel. Such requests shall be acted on in accordance with R.C.M. 506(b).

(C) *Civilian counsel.* The accused may be represented by civilian counsel at no expense to the United States. Upon request, the accused is entitled to a reasonable time to obtain civilian counsel and to have such counsel present for the preliminary hearing. However, the preliminary hearing shall not be unduly delayed for this purpose. Representation by civilian counsel shall not limit the rights to military counsel under subsections (d)(3)(A) and (B) of this rule.

(4) *Others*. The convening authority who directed the preliminary hearing may also, as a matter of discretion, detail or request an appropriate authority to detail:

(A) A reporter; and

(B) An interpreter.

(e) *Scope of preliminary hearing.*

(1) The preliminary hearing officer shall limit the inquiry to the examination of evidence, including witnesses, necessary to:

(A) Determine whether there is probable cause to believe an offense or offenses have been committed and whether the accused committed it;

(B) Determine whether a court-martial would have jurisdiction over the offense(s) and the accused;

(C) Consider whether the form of the charge(s) is proper; and

(D) Make a recommendation as to the disposition of the charge(s).

(2) If evidence adduced during the preliminary hearing indicates that the accused committed any uncharged offense(s), the preliminary hearing officer may examine evidence and hear witnesses relating to the subject matter of such offense(s) and make the findings and recommendations enumerated in subsection (e)(1) of this rule regarding such offense(s) without the accused first having been charged with the offense. The accused's rights under subsection (f)(2) of this rule, and, where it would not cause undue delay to the proceedings, subsection (g) of this rule, are the same with regard to both charged and uncharged offenses. When considering uncharged offenses identified during the preliminary hearing, the preliminary hearing officer shall inform the accused of the general nature of each uncharged offense considered, and

otherwise afford the accused the same opportunity for representation, cross examination, and presentation afforded during the preliminary hearing of any charged offense.

(f) *Rights of the accused.*

(1) Prior to any preliminary hearing under this rule the accused shall have the right to:

(A) Notice of any witnesses that the government intends to call at the preliminary hearing and copies of or access to any written or recorded statements made by those witnesses that relate to the subject matter of any charged offense;

(i) For purposes of this rule, a "written statement" is one that is signed or otherwise adopted or approved by the witness that is within the possession or control of counsel for the government; and

(ii) For purposes of this rule, a "recorded statement" is an oral statement made by the witness that is recorded contemporaneously with the making of the oral statement and contained in a digital or other recording or a transcription thereof that is within the possession or control of counsel for the government.

(B) Notice of, and reasonable access to, any other evidence that the government intends to offer at the preliminary hearing; and

(C) Notice of, and reasonable access to, evidence that is within the possession or control of counsel for the government that negates or reduces the degree of guilt of the accused for an offense charged.

(2) At any preliminary hearing under this rule the accused shall have the right to:

(A) Be advised of the charges under consideration;

(B) Be represented by counsel;

(C) Be informed of the purpose of the preliminary hearing;

(D) Be informed of the right against self-incrimination under Article 31;

(E) Except in the circumstances described in R.C.M. 804(c)(2), be present throughout the taking of evidence;

(F) Cross-examine witnesses on matters relevant to the limited scope and purpose of the preliminary hearing;

(G) Present matters in defense and mitigation relevant to the limited scope and purpose of the preliminary hearing; and

(H) Make a statement relevant to the limited scope and purpose of the preliminary hearing.

(g) *Production of Witnesses and Other Evidence.*

(1) *Military Witnesses.*

(A) Prior to the preliminary hearing, defense counsel shall provide to counsel for the government the names of proposed military witnesses whom the accused requests that the government produce to testify at the preliminary hearing, and the requested form of the testimony, in accordance with the timeline established by the preliminary hearing officer. Counsel for the government shall respond that either: (1) the government agrees that the witness's testimony is relevant, not cumulative, and necessary for the limited scope and purpose of the preliminary hearing and will seek to secure the witness's testimony for the hearing; or (2) the government objects to the proposed defense witness on the grounds that the testimony would be irrelevant, cumulative, or unnecessary based on the limited scope and purpose of the preliminary hearing.

(B) If the government objects to the proposed defense witness, defense counsel may request that the preliminary hearing officer determine whether the witness is relevant, not cumulative, and necessary based on the limited scope and purpose of the preliminary hearing.

(C) If the government does not object to the proposed defense military witness or the preliminary hearing officer determines that the military witness is relevant, not cumulative, and necessary, counsel for the government shall request that the commanding officer of the proposed military witness make that person available to provide testimony. The commanding officer shall determine whether the individual is available based on operational necessity or mission requirements, except that a victim, as defined in this rule, who declines to testify shall be deemed to be not available. If the commanding officer determines that the military witness is available, counsel for the government shall make arrangements for that individual's testimony. The commanding officer's determination of unavailability due to operational necessity or mission requirements is final. If there is a dispute among the parties, the military witness's commanding officer shall determine whether the witness testifies in person, by video teleconference, by telephone, or by similar means of remote testimony.

(2) *Civilian Witnesses.*

(A) Defense counsel shall provide to counsel for the government the names of proposed civilian witnesses whom the accused requests that the government produce to testify at the preliminary hearing, and the requested form of the testimony, in accordance with the timeline established by the preliminary hearing officer. Counsel for the government shall respond that either: (1) the government agrees that the witness's testimony is relevant, not cumulative, and necessary for the limited scope and purpose of the preliminary hearing and will seek to secure the witness's testimony for the hearing; or (2) the government objects to the proposed defense witness on the grounds that the testimony would be irrelevant, cumulative, or unnecessary based on the limited scope and purpose of the preliminary hearing.

(B) If the government objects to the proposed defense witness, defense counsel may request that the preliminary hearing officer determine whether the witness is relevant, not cumulative, and necessary based on the limited scope and purpose of the preliminary hearing.

(C) If the government does not object to the proposed civilian witness or the preliminary hearing officer determines that the civilian witness's testimony is relevant, not cumulative, and necessary, counsel for the government shall invite the civilian witness to provide testimony and, if the individual agrees, shall make arrangements for that witness's testimony. If expense to the government is to be incurred, the convening authority who directed the preliminary hearing, or the convening authority's delegate, shall determine whether the witness testifies in person, by video teleconference, by telephone, or by similar means of remote testimony.

(3) *Other evidence.*

(A) *Evidence under the control of the government.*

(i) Prior to the preliminary hearing, defense counsel shall provide to counsel for the government a list of evidence under the control of the government the accused requests the government produce to the defense for introduction at the preliminary hearing. The preliminary hearing officer may set a deadline by which defense requests must be received. Counsel for the government shall respond that either: (1) the government agrees that the evidence is relevant, not cumulative, and necessary for the limited scope and purpose of the preliminary hearing and shall make reasonable efforts to obtain the evidence; or (2) the government objects to production of the evidence on the grounds that the evidence would be irrelevant, cumulative, or unnecessary based on the limited scope and purpose of the preliminary hearing.

(ii) If the government objects to production of the evidence, defense counsel may request that the preliminary hearing officer determine whether the evidence should be produced.

The preliminary hearing officer shall determine whether the evidence is relevant, not cumulative, and necessary based on the limited scope and purpose of the hearing. If the preliminary hearing officer determines that the evidence shall be produced, counsel for the government shall make reasonable efforts to obtain the evidence.

(B) *Evidence not under the control of the government.*

(i) Evidence not under the control of the government may be obtained through noncompulsory means or by *subpoenas duces tecum* issued by counsel for the government in accordance with the process established by R.C.M. 703.

(ii) Prior to the preliminary hearing, defense counsel shall provide to counsel for the government a list of evidence not under the control of the government that the accused requests the government obtain. The preliminary hearing officer may set a deadline by which defense requests must be received. Counsel for the government shall respond that either: (1) the government agrees that the evidence is relevant, not cumulative, and necessary for the limited scope and purpose of the preliminary hearing and shall issue *subpoenas duces tecum* for the evidence; or (2) the government objects to production of the evidence on the grounds that the evidence would be irrelevant, cumulative, or unnecessary based on the limited scope and purpose of the preliminary hearing.

(iii) If the government objects to production of the evidence, defense counsel may request that the preliminary hearing officer determine whether the evidence should be produced. If the preliminary hearing officer determines that the evidence is relevant, not cumulative, and necessary based on the limited scope and purpose of the preliminary hearing and that the issuance of *subpoenas duces tecum* would not cause undue delay to the preliminary hearing, the preliminary hearing officer shall direct counsel for the government to issue *subpoenas duces tecum* for the defense-requested evidence. The preliminary hearing officer shall note in the report of preliminary hearing any failure on the part of counsel for the government to issue *subpoenas duces tecum* directed by the preliminary hearing officer.

(h) *Military Rules of Evidence.* The Military Rules of Evidence do not apply in preliminary hearings under this rule except as follows:

(1) Mil. R. Evid. 301-303 and 305 shall apply in their entirety.

(2) Mil. R. Evid. 412 shall apply in any case that includes a charge defined as a sexual offense in Mil. R. Evid. 412(d), except that Mil. R. Evid. 412(b)(1)(C) shall not apply.

(3) Mil. R. Evid., Section V, Privileges, shall apply, except that Mil. R. Evid. 505(f)-(h) and (j); 506(f)-(h), (j), (k), and (m); and 514(d)(6) shall not apply.

(4) In applying these rules to a preliminary hearing, the term "military judge," as used in these rules, shall mean the preliminary hearing officer, who shall assume the military judge's authority to exclude evidence from the preliminary hearing, and who shall, in discharging this duty, follow the procedures set forth in the rules cited in subsections (h)(1)-(3) of this rule. However, the preliminary hearing officer is not authorized to order production of communications covered by Mil. R. Evid. 513 and 514.

(5) Failure to meet the procedural requirements of the applicable rules of evidence shall result in exclusion of that evidence from the preliminary hearing, unless good cause is shown.

(i) *Procedure.*

(1) *Generally.* The preliminary hearing shall begin with the preliminary hearing officer informing the accused of the accused's rights under subsection (f) of this rule. Counsel for the government will then present evidence. Upon the conclusion of counsel for the government's presentation of evidence, defense counsel may present matters in defense and mitigation

consistent with subsection (f) of this rule. For the purposes of this rule, "matters in mitigation" are defined as matters that may serve to explain the circumstances surrounding a charged offense. Both counsel for the government and defense shall be afforded an opportunity to cross-examine adverse witnesses. The preliminary hearing officer may also question witnesses called by the parties. If the preliminary hearing officer determines that additional evidence is necessary to satisfy the requirements of subsection (e) of this rule, the preliminary hearing officer may provide the parties an opportunity to present additional testimony or evidence relevant to the limited scope and purpose of the preliminary hearing. The preliminary hearing officer shall not consider evidence not presented at the preliminary hearing. The preliminary hearing officer shall not call witnesses *sua sponte*.

(2) *Notice to and presence of the victim(s)*.

(A) The victim(s) of an offense under the UCMJ has the right to reasonable, accurate, and timely notice of a preliminary hearing relating to the alleged offense and the reasonable right to confer with counsel for the government. For the purposes of this rule, a "victim" is a person who is alleged to have suffered a direct physical, emotional, or pecuniary harm as a result of the matters set forth in a charge or specification under consideration and is named in one of the specifications under consideration.

(B) A victim of an offense under consideration at the preliminary hearing is not required to testify at the preliminary hearing.

(C) A victim has the right not to be excluded from any portion of a preliminary hearing related to the alleged offense, unless the preliminary hearing officer, after receiving clear and convincing evidence, determines the testimony by the victim would be materially altered if the victim heard other testimony at the proceeding.

(D) A victim shall be excluded if a privilege set forth in Mil. R. Evid. 505 or 506 is invoked or if evidence is offered under Mil. R. Evid. 412, 513, or 514, for charges other than those in which the victim is named.

(3) *Presentation of evidence.*

(A) *Testimony.* Witness testimony may be provided in person, by video teleconference, by telephone, or by similar means of remote testimony. All testimony shall be taken under oath, except that the accused may make an unsworn statement. The preliminary hearing officer shall only consider testimony that is relevant to the limited scope and purpose of the preliminary hearing.

(B) *Other evidence.* If relevant to the limited scope and purpose of the preliminary hearing, and not cumulative, a preliminary hearing officer may consider other evidence, in addition to or in lieu of witness testimony, including statements, tangible evidence, or reproductions thereof, offered by either side, that the preliminary hearing officer determines is reliable. This other evidence need not be sworn.

(4) *Access by spectators.* Preliminary hearings are public proceedings and should remain open to the public whenever possible. The convening authority who directed the preliminary hearing or the preliminary hearing officer may restrict or foreclose access by spectators to all or part of the proceedings if an overriding interest exists that outweighs the value of an open preliminary hearing. Examples of overriding interests may include: preventing psychological harm or trauma to a child witness or an alleged victim of a sexual crime, protecting the safety or privacy of a witness or alleged victim, protecting classified material, and receiving evidence where a witness is incapable of testifying in an open setting. Any closure must be narrowly tailored to achieve the overriding interest that justified the closure. Convening authorities or preliminary hearing

officers must conclude that no lesser methods short of closing the preliminary hearing can be used to protect the overriding interest in the case. Convening authorities or preliminary hearing officers must conduct a case-by-case, witness-by-witness, circumstance-by-circumstance analysis of whether closure is necessary. If a convening authority or preliminary hearing officer believes closing the preliminary hearing is necessary, the convening authority or preliminary hearing officer must make specific findings of fact in writing that support the closure. The written findings of fact must be included in the report of preliminary hearing.

(5) *Presence of accused.* The further progress of the taking of evidence shall not be prevented and the accused shall be considered to have waived the right to be present whenever the accused:

(A) After being notified of the time and place of the proceeding is voluntarily absent; or

(B) After being warned by the preliminary hearing officer that disruptive conduct will cause removal from the proceeding, persists in conduct that is such as to justify exclusion from the proceeding.

(6) *Recording of the preliminary hearing.* Counsel for the government shall ensure that the preliminary hearing is recorded by a suitable recording device. A victim, as defined by subsection (i)(2)(A) of this rule, may request access to, or a copy of, the recording of the proceedings. Upon request, counsel for the government shall provide the requested access to, or a copy of, the recording to the victim not later than a reasonable time following dismissal of the charges, unless charges are dismissed for the purpose of re-referral, or court-martial adjournment. A victim is not entitled to classified information or access to or a copy of a recording of closed sessions that the victim did not have the right to attend under subsections (i)(2)(C) or (i)(2)(D) of this rule.

(7) *Objections.* Any objection alleging a failure to comply with this rule shall be made to the convening authority via the preliminary hearing officer.

(8) *Sealed exhibits and proceedings.* The preliminary hearing officer has the authority to order exhibits, proceedings, or other matters sealed as described in R.C.M. 1103A.

(j) *Report of preliminary hearing.*

(1) *In general.* The preliminary hearing officer shall make a timely written report of the preliminary hearing to the convening authority who directed the preliminary hearing.

(2) *Contents.* The report of preliminary hearing shall include:

(A) A statement of names and organizations or addresses of defense counsel and whether defense counsel was present throughout the taking of evidence, or, if not present, the reason why;

(B) The substance of the testimony taken on both sides;

(C) Any other statements, documents, or matters considered by the preliminary hearing officer, or recitals of the substance or nature of such evidence;

(D) A statement that an essential witness may not be available for trial;

(E) An explanation of any delays in the preliminary hearing;

(F) A notation if counsel for the government failed to issue a *subpoena duces tecum* that was directed by the preliminary hearing officer;

(G) The preliminary hearing officer's determination as to whether there is probable cause to believe the offense(s) listed on the charge sheet or otherwise considered at the preliminary hearing occurred;

(H) The preliminary hearing officer's determination as to whether there is probable cause to believe the accused committed the offense(s) listed on the charge sheet or otherwise considered at the preliminary hearing;

(I) The preliminary hearing officer's determination as to whether a court-martial has jurisdiction over the offense(s) and the accused;

(J) The preliminary hearing officer's determination as to whether the charge(s) and specification(s) are in proper form; and

(K) The preliminary hearing officer's recommendations regarding disposition of the charge(s).

(3) *Sealed exhibits and proceedings.* If the report of preliminary hearing contains exhibits, proceedings, or other matters ordered sealed by the preliminary hearing officer in accordance with R.C.M. 1103A, counsel for the government shall cause such materials to be sealed so as to prevent unauthorized viewing or disclosure.

(4) *Distribution of the report.* The preliminary hearing officer shall cause the report to be delivered to the convening authority who directed the preliminary hearing. That convening authority shall promptly cause a copy of the report to be delivered to each accused.

(5) *Objections.* Any objection to the report shall be made to the convening authority who directed the preliminary hearing, via the preliminary hearing officer. Upon receipt of the report, the accused has 5 days to submit objections to the preliminary hearing officer. The preliminary hearing officer will forward the objections to the convening authority as soon as practicable. This subsection does not prohibit a convening authority from referring the charge(s) or taking other action within the 5-day period.

(k) *Waiver.* The accused may waive a preliminary hearing under this rule. However, the convening authority authorized to direct the preliminary hearing may direct that it be conducted notwithstanding the waiver. Failure to make a timely objection under this rule, including an objection to the report, shall constitute waiver of the objection. Relief from the waiver may be granted by the convening authority who directed the preliminary hearing, a superior convening authority, or the military judge, as appropriate, for good cause shown."

(l) R.C.M. 601(g) is inserted immediately after R.C.M. 601(f) and reads as follows:

"(g) *Parallel convening authorities*. If it is impracticable for the original convening authority to continue exercising authority over the charges, the convening authority may cause the charges, even if referred, to be transmitted to a parallel convening authority. This transmittal must be in writing and in accordance with such regulations as the Secretary concerned may prescribe. Subsequent actions taken by the parallel convening authority are within the sole discretion of that convening authority."

(m) R.C.M. 702(a) is amended to read as follows:

"(a) *In general*. A deposition may be ordered whenever, after preferral of charges, due to exceptional circumstances of the case it is in the interest of justice that the testimony of a prospective witness be taken and preserved for use at a preliminary hearing under Article 32 or a court-martial. A victim's declination to testify at a preliminary hearing or a victim's declination to submit to pretrial interviews shall not, by themselves, be considered exceptional circumstances. In accordance with subsection (b) of this rule, the convening authority or military judge may order a deposition of a victim only if it is determined, by a preponderance of the evidence, that the victim will not be available to testify at court-martial."

(n) R.C.M. 702(c)(2) is amended to read as follows:

"(2) *Contents of request*. A request for a deposition shall include:

(A) The name and address of the person whose deposition is requested, or, if the name of the person is unknown, a description of the office or position of the person;

(B) A statement of the matters on which the person is to be examined; and

(C) Whether an oral or written deposition is requested."

(o) R.C.M. 702(c)(3)(A) is amended to read as follows:

"(A) Upon receipt of a request for a deposition, the convening authority or military judge shall determine whether the requesting party has shown, by a preponderance of the evidence, that due to exceptional circumstances and in the interest of justice, the testimony of the prospective witness must be taken and preserved for use at a preliminary hearing under Article 32 or court-martial."

(p) R.C.M. 702(d)(1) is amended to read as follows:

"(1) *Detail of deposition officer.* When a request for a deposition is approved, the convening authority shall detail a judge advocate certified under Article 27(b) to serve as deposition officer. When the appointment of a judge advocate as deposition officer is not practicable, the convening authority may detail an impartial commissioned officer or appropriate civil officer authorized to administer oaths, not the accuser, to serve as deposition officer. If the deposition officer is not a judge advocate, an impartial judge advocate certified under Article 27(b) shall be made available to provide legal advice to the deposition officer."

(q) R.C.M. 703(e)(2)(B) is amended to read as follows:

"(B) *Contents.* A subpoena shall state the command by which the proceeding is directed, and the title, if any, of the proceeding. A subpoena shall command each person to whom it is directed to attend and give testimony at the time and place specified therein. A subpoena may also command the person to whom it is directed to produce books, papers, documents, data, or other objects or electronically stored information designated therein at the proceeding or at an earlier time for inspection by the parties. A subpoena issued for a preliminary hearing pursuant to Article 32 shall not command any person to attend or give testimony at an Article 32 preliminary hearing."

(r) R.C.M. 703(e)(2)(C) is amended to read as follows:

"(C) *Who may issue.*

(1) A subpoena to secure evidence may be issued by:

(a) The summary court-martial;

(b) At an Article 32 preliminary hearing, detailed counsel for the government;

(c) After referral to a court-martial, detailed trial counsel;

(d) The president of a court of inquiry; or

(e) An officer detailed to take a deposition."

(s) R.C.M. 703(f)(4)(B) is amended to read as follows:

"(B) *Evidence not under the control of the government.* Evidence not under the control of the government may be obtained by a subpoena issued in accordance with subsection (e)(2) of this rule. A *subpoena duces tecum* to produce books, papers, documents, data, or other objects or electronically stored information for a preliminary hearing pursuant to Article 32 may be issued, following the convening authority's order directing such preliminary hearing, by counsel for the government. A person in receipt of a *subpoena duces tecum* for an Article 32 hearing need not personally appear in order to comply with the subpoena."

(t) R.C.M. 801(a)(6) is inserted after R.C.M. 801(a)(5) and reads as follows:

"(6) In the case of a victim of an offense under the UCMJ who is under 18 years of age and not a member of the armed forces, or who is incompetent, incapacitated, or deceased, designate in writing a family member, a representative of the estate of the victim, or another suitable individual to assume the victim's rights under the UCMJ.

(A) For the purposes of this rule, the individual is designated for the sole purpose of assuming the legal rights of the victim as they pertain to the victim's status as a victim of any offense(s) properly before the court.

(B) *Procedure to determine appointment of designee.*

     (i) As soon as practicable, trial counsel shall notify the military judge, counsel for the accused, and the victim(s) of any offense(s) properly before the court when there is an apparent requirement to appoint a designee under this rule.

     (ii) The military judge will determine if the appointment of a designee is required under this rule.

     (iii) At the discretion of the military judge, victim(s), trial counsel, and the accused may be given the opportunity to recommend to the military judge individual(s) for appointment.

     (iv) The military judge is not required to hold a hearing before determining whether a designation is required or making such an appointment under this rule.

     (v) If the military judge determines a hearing pursuant to Article 39(a), UCMJ, is necessary, the following shall be notified of the hearing and afforded the right to be present at the hearing: trial counsel, accused, and the victim(s).

     (vi) The individual designated shall not be the accused.

(C) At any time after appointment, a designee shall be excused upon request by the designee or a finding of good cause by the military judge.

(D) If the individual appointed to assume the victim's rights is excused, the military judge shall appoint a successor consistent with this rule."

(u) A new R.C.M. 806(b)(2) is inserted immediately after R.C.M. 806(b)(1) and reads as follows:

     "(2) *Right of victim to attend.* A victim of an alleged offense committed by the accused may not be excluded from a court-martial relating to the offense unless the military judge, after receiving clear and convincing evidence, determines that testimony by the victim would be materially altered if the victim heard other testimony at that hearing or proceeding. The right to attend requires reasonable, accurate, and timely notice of a court-martial relating to the offense."

(v) A new R.C.M. 806(b)(3) is inserted immediately after the new R.C.M. 806(b)(2) and reads as follows:

"(3) *Right of victim to confer.* A victim of an alleged offense committed by the accused has the reasonable right to confer with the trial counsel."

(w) R.C.M. 806(b)(2) is renumbered as R.C.M. 806(b)(4).

(x) R.C.M. 906(b)(8) is amended to read as follows:

"(8) *Relief from pretrial confinement.* Upon a motion for release from pretrial confinement, a victim of an alleged offense committed by the accused has the right to reasonable, accurate, and timely notice of the motion and any hearing, the right to confer with trial counsel, and the right to be reasonably heard. Inability to reasonably afford a victim these rights shall not delay the proceedings. The right to be heard under this rule includes the right to be heard through counsel."

(y) R.C.M. 912(i)(3) is amended to read as follows:

"(3) *Preliminary hearing officer.* For purposes of this rule, "preliminary hearing officer" includes any person who has examined charges under R.C.M. 405 and any person who was counsel for a member of a court of inquiry, or otherwise personally has conducted an investigation of the general matter involving the offenses charged."

(z) R.C.M. 1001(a)(1)(B) is amended to read as follows:

"(B) Victim's right to be reasonably heard. *See* R.C.M. 1001A."

(aa) R.C.M. 1001(a)(1)(C)–(G) are amended to read as follows:

"(C) Presentation by the defense of evidence in extenuation or mitigation or both.

(D) Rebuttal.

(E) Argument by trial counsel on sentence.

(F) Argument by defense counsel on sentence.

(G) Rebuttal arguments in the discretion of the military judge."

(bb) A new rule, R.C.M. 1001A, is inserted immediately after R.C.M. 1001(g) and reads as follows:

"Rule 1001A. Crime victims and presentencing

(a) *In general.* A crime victim of an offense of which the accused has been found guilty has the right to be reasonably heard at a sentencing hearing relating to that offense. A victim under this rule is not considered a witness for purposes of Article 42(b). Trial counsel shall ensure the victim is aware of the opportunity to exercise that right. If the victim exercises the right to be reasonably heard, the victim shall be called by the court-martial. This right is independent of whether the victim testified during findings or is called to testify under R.C.M. 1001.

(b) *Definitions.*

(1) *Crime victim.* For purposes of this rule, a "crime victim" is an individual who has suffered direct physical, emotional, or pecuniary harm as a result of the commission of an offense of which the accused was found guilty.

(2) *Victim Impact.* For the purposes of this rule, "victim impact" includes any financial, social, psychological, or medical impact on the victim directly relating to or arising from the offense of which the accused has been found guilty.

(3) *Mitigation.* For the purposes of this rule, "mitigation" includes a matter to lessen the punishment to be adjudged by the court-martial or to furnish grounds for a recommendation of clemency.

(4) *Right to be reasonably heard.*

(A) *Capital cases.* In capital cases, for purposes of this rule, the "right to be reasonably heard" means the right to make a sworn statement.

(B) *Non-capital cases.* In non-capital cases, for purposes of this rule, the "right to be reasonably heard" means the right to make a sworn or unsworn statement.

(c) *Content of statement.* The content of statements made under subsections (d) and (e) of this rule may include victim impact or matters in mitigation.

(d) *Sworn statement.* The victim may give a sworn statement under this rule and shall be subject to cross-examination concerning the statement by the trial counsel or defense counsel or examination on the statement by the court-martial, or all or any of the three. When a victim is under 18 years of age, incompetent, incapacitated, or deceased, the sworn statement may be made by the victim's designee appointed under R.C.M. 801(a)(6). Additionally, a victim under 18 years of age may elect to make a sworn statement.

(e) *Unsworn statement.* The victim may make an unsworn statement and may not be cross-examined by the trial counsel or defense counsel upon it or examined upon it by the court-martial. The prosecution or defense may, however, rebut any statements of facts therein. The unsworn statement may be oral, written, or both. When a victim is under 18 years of age, incompetent, incapacitated, or deceased, the unsworn statement may be made by the victim's designee appointed under R.C.M. 801(a)(6). Additionally, a victim under 18 years of age may elect to make an unsworn statement.

(1) *Procedure for presenting unsworn statement.* After the announcement of findings, a victim who would like to present an unsworn statement shall provide a copy to the trial counsel, defense counsel, and military judge. The military judge may waive this requirement for good cause shown.

(2) Upon good cause shown, the military judge may permit the victim's counsel to deliver all or part of the victim's unsworn statement.

(cc) R.C.M. 1103A(a) is amended to read as follows:

"(a) *In general.* If the report of preliminary hearing or record of trial contains exhibits, proceedings, or other matter ordered sealed by the preliminary hearing officer or military judge, counsel for the government or trial counsel shall cause such materials to be sealed so as to prevent unauthorized viewing or disclosure. Counsel for the government or trial counsel shall ensure that such materials are properly marked, including an annotation that the material was sealed by order of the preliminary hearing officer or military judge, and inserted at the appropriate place in the original record of trial. Copies of the report of preliminary hearing or record of trial shall contain appropriate annotations that matters were sealed by order of the preliminary hearing officer or military judge and have been inserted in the report of preliminary hearing or original record of trial. This Rule shall be implemented in a manner consistent with Executive Order 13526, concerning classified national security information."

(dd) R.C.M. 1103A(b)(1) is amended to read as follows:

"(1) *Prior to referral.* The following individuals may examine sealed materials only if necessary for proper fulfillment of their responsibilities under the UCMJ, the MCM, governing directives, instructions, regulations, applicable rules for practice and procedure, or rules of professional responsibility: the judge advocate advising the convening authority who directed the Article 32 preliminary hearing; the convening authority who directed the Article 32 preliminary hearing; the staff judge advocate to the general court-martial convening authority; and the general court-martial convening authority."

(ee) R.C.M. 1103A(b)(5) is inserted immediately after R.C.M. 1103A(b)(4)(E)(viii) and reads as follows:

"(5) *Examination of sealed matters.* For the purpose of this rule, "examination" includes reading, viewing, photocopying, photographing, disclosing, or manipulating the sealed matters in any way."

(ff) R.C.M. 1105 is amended by inserting the following Note before the rule's heading:

"[Note: R.C.M. 1105(b)(1) and (b)(2)(C) apply to offenses committed on or after 24 June 2014.]"

(gg) R.C.M. 1105(b)(1) is amended to read as follows:

"(1) The accused may submit to the convening authority any matters that may reasonably tend to affect the convening authority's decision whether to disapprove any findings of guilty or to approve the sentence, except as may be limited by R.C.M. 1107(b)(3)(C). The convening authority is only required to consider written submissions."

(hh) R.C.M. 1105(b)(2)(C) is amended to read as follows:

"(C) Matters in mitigation that were not available for consideration at the court-martial, except as may be limited by R.C.M. 1107(b)(3)(B); and"

(ii) R.C.M. 1107 is amended by inserting the following Note before the rule's heading:

"[Note: Subsections (b)-(f) of R.C.M. 1107 apply to offenses committed on or after 24 June 2014; however, if at least one offense in a case occurred prior to 24 June 2014, then the prior version of RCM 1107 applies to all offenses in the case, except that mandatory minimum sentences under Article 56(b) and applicable rules under RCM 1107(d)(1)(D)-(E) still apply.]"

(jj) R.C.M. 1107(b)(1) is amended to read as follows:

"(1) *Discretion of convening authority.* Any action to be taken on the findings and sentence is within the sole discretion of the convening authority. The convening authority is not required to review the case for legal errors or factual sufficiency."

(kk) R.C.M. 1107(b)(3)(A)(iii) is amended to read as follows:

"(iii) Any matters submitted by the accused under R.C.M. 1105 or, if applicable, R.C.M. 1106(f);"

(ll) R.C.M. 1107(b)(3)(A)(iv) is amended to read as follows:

"(iv) Any statement submitted by a crime victim pursuant to R.C.M. 1105A and subsection (C) of this rule."

(mm) R.C.M. 1107(b)(3)(B)(i) is amended to read as follows:

"(i) The record of trial, subject to the provisions of R.C.M. 1103A and subsection (C) of this rule;"

(nn) R.C.M. 1107(c) is amended to read as follows:

"(c) *Action on findings.* Action on the findings is not required. However, the convening authority may take action subject to the following limitations:

(1) For offenses charged under subsection (a) or (b) of Article 120, offenses charged under Article 120b, and offenses charged under Article 125:

(A) The convening authority is prohibited from:

(i) Setting aside any finding of guilt or dismissing a specification; or

(ii) Changing a finding of guilty to a charge or specification to a finding of guilty to an offense that is a lesser included offense of the offense stated in the charge or specification.

(B) The convening authority may direct a rehearing in accordance with subsection (e) of this rule.

(2) For offenses other than those listed in subsection (c)(1) of this rule for which the maximum sentence of confinement that may be adjudged does not exceed two years without regard to the jurisdictional limits of the court, and the sentence adjudged does not include dismissal, a dishonorable discharge, bad-conduct discharge, or confinement for more than six months:

(A) The convening authority may change a finding of guilty to a charge or specification to a finding of guilty to an offense that is a lesser included offense of the offense stated in the charge or specification; or

(B) Set aside any finding of guilty and:

(i) Dismiss the specification and, if appropriate, the charge; or

(ii) Direct a rehearing in accordance with subsection (e) of this rule.

(3) If the convening authority acts to dismiss or change any charge or specification for an offense, the convening authority shall provide, at the same time, a written explanation of the reasons for such action. The written explanation shall be made a part of the record of trial and action thereon."

(oo) R.C.M. 1107(d)(1) is amended to read as follows:

"(1) *In general.*

(A) The convening authority may not disapprove, commute, or suspend, in whole or in part, any portion of an adjudged sentence of confinement for more than six months.

(B) The convening authority may not disapprove, commute, or suspend that portion of an adjudged sentence that includes a dismissal, dishonorable discharge, or bad-conduct discharge.

(C) The convening authority may disapprove, commute, or suspend, in whole or in part, any portion of an adjudged sentence when doing so is not explicitly prohibited by this Rule.

Actions affecting reduction in pay grade, forfeitures of pay and allowances, fines, reprimands, restrictions, and hard labor without confinement are not explicitly prohibited by this Rule.

(D) The convening authority shall not disapprove, commute, or suspend any mandatory minimum sentence of dismissal or dishonorable discharge except in accordance with subsection (E) of this Rule.

(E) *Exceptions.*

(i) *Trial counsel recommendation.* Upon the recommendation of the trial counsel, in recognition of the substantial assistance by the accused in the investigation or prosecution of another person who has committed an offense, the convening authority or another person authorized to act under this section shall have the authority to disapprove, commute, or suspend the adjudged sentence, in whole or in part, even with respect to an offense for which a mandatory minimum sentence exists.

(ii) *Pretrial agreement.* If a pretrial agreement has been entered into by the convening authority and the accused as authorized by R.C.M. 705, the convening authority shall have the authority to approve, disapprove, commute, or suspend a sentence, in whole or in part, pursuant to the terms of the pretrial agreement. The convening authority may commute a mandatory sentence of a dishonorable discharge to a bad-conduct discharge pursuant to the terms of the pretrial agreement.

(F) If the convening authority acts to disapprove, commute, or suspend, in whole or in part, the sentence of the court-martial for an offense, the convening authority shall provide, at the same time, a written explanation of the reasons for such action. The written explanation shall be made a part of the record of trial and action thereon."

(pp) R.C.M. 1107(d)(2) is amended to read as follows:

"(2) *Determining what sentence should be approved.* The convening authority shall, subject to the limitations in subsection (d)(1) above, approve that sentence that is warranted by the circumstances of the offense and appropriate for the accused."

(qq) R.C.M. 1107(e)(1)(B)(ii) is amended to read as follows:

"(ii) In cases subject to review by the Court of Criminal Appeals, before the case is forwarded under R.C.M. 1111(a)(1) or (b)(1), but only as to any sentence that was approved or findings of guilty as were not disapproved in any earlier action. In cases of rehearing under subparagraph (c)(2) of this Rule, a supplemental action disapproving the sentence and some or all of the findings , as appropriate, shall be taken; or"

(rr) R.C.M. 1107(e)(1)(C)(ii) is deleted.

(ss) R.C.M. 1107(e)(1)(C)(iii) is renumbered as R.C.M. 1107(e)(1)(C)(ii).

(tt) R.C.M. 1107(f)(2) is amended to read as follows:

"(2) *Modification of initial action.* Subject to the limitations in subsections (c) and (d) of this Rule, the convening authority may recall and modify any action taken by that convening authority at any time before it has been published or before the accused has been officially notified. The convening authority may also recall and modify any action at any time prior to forwarding the record for review, as long as the modification does not result in action less favorable to the accused than the earlier action. In addition, in any special court-martial, the convening authority may recall and correct an illegal, erroneous, incomplete, or ambiguous action at any time before completion of review under R.C.M. 1112, as long as the correction does not result in action less favorable to the accused than the earlier action. When so directed by a higher reviewing authority or the Judge Advocate General, the convening authority shall modify any incomplete, ambiguous, void, or inaccurate action noted in review of the record of trial under Articles 64, 66, 67, or examination of the record of trial under Article 69. The convening authority shall personally sign any supplementary or corrective action. A written explanation is required for any modification of initial action that: 1) sets aside any finding of guilt or dismisses or changes any charge or specification for an offense; or 2) disapproves, commutes, or suspends, in whole or in part, the sentence. The written explanation shall be made a part of the record of trial and action thereon."

(uu) R.C.M. 1107(g) is amended to read as follows:

"(g) *Incomplete, ambiguous, or erroneous action.* When the action of the convening authority or of a higher authority is incomplete or ambiguous or contains error, the authority who took the incomplete, ambiguous, or erroneous action may be instructed by an authority acting under Articles 64, 66, 67, 67a, or 69 to withdraw the original action and substitute a corrected action."

(vv) R.C.M. 1108(b) is amended to insert the following before the rule's text:

"[Note: R.C.M. 1108(b) applies to offenses committed on or after 24 June 2014.]"

(ww) R.C.M. 1108(b) is amended to read as follows:

"(b) *Who may suspend and remit.* The convening authority may, after approving the sentence, suspend the execution of all or any part of the sentence of a court-martial, except for a sentence of death or as prohibited under R.C.M. 1107(d). The general court-martial convening authority over the accused at the time of the court-martial may, when taking action under R.C.M. 1112(f), suspend or remit any part of the sentence. The Secretary concerned and, when designated by the Secretary concerned, any Under Secretary, Assistant Secretary, Judge Advocate General, or commanding officer may suspend or remit any part or amount of the unexecuted part of any sentence other than a sentence approved by the President or a sentence of confinement for life without eligibility for parole that has been ordered executed. The Secretary concerned may, however, suspend or remit the unexecuted part of a sentence of confinement for life without eligibility for parole after the service of a period of confinement of not less than 20 years. The commander of the accused who has the authority to convene a court-martial of the kind that adjudged the sentence may suspend or remit any part of the unexecuted part of any sentence by summary court-martial or of any sentence by special court-martial that does not include a bad-conduct discharge regardless of whether the person acting has previously approved the sentence. The "unexecuted part of any sentence" is that part that has been approved and ordered executed but that has not actually been carried out."

(xx) R.C.M. 1301(c) is amended to insert the following before the rule's text:

"[Note: R.C.M. 1301(c) applies to offenses committed on or after 24 June 2014.]"

(yy) R.C.M. 1301(c) is amended to number the current paragraph as (1), and a new R.C.M. 1301(c)(2) is inserted after the new R.C.M. 1301(c)(1) and reads as follows:

"(2) Notwithstanding subsection (c)(1) of this Rule, summary courts-martial do not have jurisdiction over offenses under Articles 120(a), 120(b), 120b(a), 120b(b), forcible sodomy under Article 125, and attempts thereof under Article 80. Such offenses shall not be referred to a summary court-martial."

(zz) R.C.M. 406(b)(2) and R.C.M. 1103 are amended by changing "report of investigation" to "report of preliminary hearing".

(aaa) R.C.M. 603(b) and R.C.M. 912(f)(1)(F) are amended by changing "an investigating officer" to "a preliminary hearing officer".

(bbb) R.C.M. 705(c)(2)(E), R.C.M. 905(b)(1), and R.C.M. 906(b)(3) are amended by changing "Article 32 investigation" to "Article 32 preliminary hearing".

(ccc) R.C.M. 706(a), R.C.M. 706(c)(3)(A), R.C.M. 902(b)(2), R.C.M. 912(a)(1)(K), R.C.M. 1106(b), and R.C.M. 1112(c) are amended by changing "investigating officer" to "preliminary hearing officer".

Sec. 2. Part III of the Manual for Courts-Martial, United States, is amended as follows:

(a) Mil. R. Evid. 404(a)(2)(A) is amended to read as follows:

"(A) The accused may offer evidence of the accused's pertinent trait and, if the evidence is admitted, the prosecution may offer evidence to rebut it. General military character is not a pertinent trait for the purposes of showing the probability of innocence of the accused for the following offenses under the UCMJ:

(i) Articles 120–123a;

(ii) Articles 125–127;

(iii) Articles 129–132;

(iv) Any other offense in which evidence of general military character of the accused is not relevant to any element of an offense for which the accused has been charged; or

(v) An attempt or conspiracy to commit one of the above offenses."

(b) Mil. R. Evid. 412(c)(2) is amended to read as follows:

"(2) Before admitting evidence under this rule, the military judge must conduct a hearing, which shall be closed. At this hearing, the parties may call witnesses, including the alleged victim, and offer relevant evidence. The alleged victim must be afforded a reasonable opportunity to attend and be heard. However, the hearing may not be unduly delayed for this purpose. The right to be heard under this rule includes the right to be heard through counsel, including Special Victims' Counsel under section 1044e of title 10, United States Code. In a case before a court-martial composed of a military judge and members, the military judge shall conduct the hearing outside the presence of the members pursuant to Article 39(a). The motion, related papers, and the record of the hearing must be sealed in accordance with R.C.M. 1103A and remain under seal unless the military judge or an appellate court orders otherwise."

(c) Mil. R. Evid. 513(b)(2) is amended to read as follows:

"(2) "Psychotherapist" means a psychiatrist, clinical psychologist, clinical social worker, or other mental health professional who is licensed in any State, territory, possession, the District of Columbia, or Puerto Rico to perform professional services as such, or who holds credentials to provide such services as such, or who holds credentials to provide such services from any military health care facility, or is a person reasonably believed by the patient to have such license or credentials."

(d) Mil. R. Evid. 513(d)(8) is deleted.

(e) Mil. R. Evid. 513(e)(2) is amended to read as follows:

"(2) Before ordering the production or admission of evidence of a patient's records or communication, the military judge must conduct a hearing, which shall be closed. At the hearing, the parties may call witnesses, including the patient, and offer other relevant evidence. The patient must be afforded a reasonable opportunity to attend the hearing and be heard. However, the hearing may not be unduly delayed for this purpose. The right to be heard under this rule includes the right to be heard through counsel, including Special Victims' Counsel under section 1044e of title 10, United States Code. In a case before a court-martial composed of a military judge and members, the military judge must conduct the hearing outside the presence of the members."

(f) Mil. R. Evid. 513(e)(3) is amended to read as follows:

"(3) The military judge may examine the evidence or a proffer thereof in camera, if such examination is necessary to rule on the production or admissibility of protected records or communications. Prior to conducting an in camera review, the military judge must find by a preponderance of the evidence that the moving party showed:

(A) a specific factual basis demonstrating a reasonable likelihood that the records or communications would yield evidence admissible under an exception to the privilege;

(B) that the requested information meets one of the enumerated exceptions under subsection (d) of this rule;

(C) that the information sought is not merely cumulative of other information available; and

(D) that the party made reasonable efforts to obtain the same or substantially similar information through non-privileged sources."

(g) A new Mil. R. Evid. 513(e)(4) is inserted immediately after Mil. R. Evid. 513(e)(3) and reads as follows:

"(4) Any production or disclosure permitted by the military judge under this rule must be narrowly tailored to only the specific records or communications, or portions of such records or communications, that meet the requirements for one of the enumerated exceptions to the privilege under subsection (d) of this Rule and are included in the stated purpose for which the records or communications are sought under subsection (e)(1)(A) of this Rule."

(h) Mil. R. Evid. 513(e)(4) is renumbered as Mil. R. Evid. 513(e)(5).

(i) Mil. R. Evid. 513(e)(5) is renumbered as Mil. R. Evid. 513(e)(6).

(j) The title of Mil. R. Evid. 514 is amended to read as follows:

"Victim advocate-victim and Department of Defense Safe Helpline staff-victim privilege"

(k) Mil. R. Evid. 514(a) is amended to read as follows:

"(a) *General Rule.* A victim has a privilege to refuse to disclose and to prevent any other person from disclosing a confidential communication made between the alleged victim and a victim advocate or between the alleged victim and Department of Defense Safe Helpline staff, in a case arising under the UCMJ, if such communication was made for the purpose of facilitating advice or assistance to the alleged victim."

(l) Mil. R. Evid. 514(b)(3)-(5) is amended to read as follows

"(3) "Department of Defense Safe Helpline staff" are persons who are designated by competent authority in writing as Department of Defense Safe Helpline staff.

(4) A communication is "confidential" if made in the course of the victim advocate-victim relationship or Department of Defense Safe Helpline staff-victim relationship and not intended to be disclosed to third persons other than those to whom disclosure is made in furtherance of the rendition of advice or assistance to the alleged victim or those reasonably necessary for such transmission of the communication.

(5) "Evidence of a victim's records or communications" means testimony of a victim advocate or Department of Defense Safe Helpline staff, or records that pertain to communications by a victim to a victim advocate or Department of Defense Safe Helpline staff, for the purposes of advising or providing assistance to the victim."

(m) Mil. R. Evid. 514(c) is amended to read as follows:

"(c) *Who May Claim the Privilege*. The privilege may be claimed by the victim or the guardian or conservator of the victim. A person who may claim the privilege may authorize trial counsel or a counsel representing the victim to claim the privilege on his or her behalf. The victim advocate or Department of Defense Safe Helpline staff who received the communication may claim the privilege on behalf of the victim. The authority of such a victim advocate, Department of Defense Safe Helpline staff, guardian, conservator, or a counsel representing the victim to so assert the privilege is presumed in the absence of evidence to the contrary."

(n) Mil. R. Evid. 514(d)(2)-(4) is amended to read as follows:

"(2) When federal law, state law, Department of Defense regulation, or service regulation imposes a duty to report information contained in a communication;

(3) When a victim advocate or Department of Defense Safe Helpline staff believes that a victim's mental or emotional condition makes the victim a danger to any person, including the victim;

(4) If the communication clearly contemplated the future commission of a fraud or crime, or if the services of the victim advocate or Department of Defense Safe Helpline staff are sought or obtained to enable or aid anyone to commit or plan to commit what the victim knew or reasonably should have known to be a crime or fraud;"

(o) Mil. R. Evid. 514(e)(2) is amended to read as follows:

"(2) Before ordering the production or admission of evidence of a victim's records or communication, the military judge must conduct a hearing, which shall be closed. At the hearing, the parties may call witnesses, including the victim, and offer other relevant evidence. The victim must be afforded a reasonable opportunity to attend the hearing and be heard. However, the hearing may not be unduly delayed for this purpose. The right to be heard under this rule includes the right to be heard through counsel, including Special Victims' Counsel under section 1044e of title 10, United States Code. In a case before a court-martial composed of a military judge and members, the military judge must conduct the hearing outside the presence of the members."

(p) Mil. R. Evid. 514(e)(3) is amended to read as follows:

"(3) The military judge may examine the evidence, or a proffer thereof, in camera if such examination is necessary to rule on the production or admissibility of protected records or communications. Prior to conducting an in camera review, the military judge must find by a preponderance of the evidence that the moving party showed:

(A) a specific factual basis demonstrating a reasonable likelihood that the records or communications would yield evidence admissible under an exception to the privilege;

(B) that the requested information meets one of the enumerated exceptions under subsection (d) of this rule;

(C) that the information sought is not merely cumulative of other information available; and

(D) that the party made reasonable efforts to obtain the same or substantially similar information through non-privileged sources."

(q) A new Mil. R. Evid. 514(e)(4) is inserted immediately after Mil. R. Evid. 514(e)(3) and reads as follows:

"(4) Any production or disclosure permitted by the military judge under this rule must be narrowly tailored to only the specific records or communications, or portions of such records or communications, that meet the requirements for one of the enumerated exceptions to the privilege under subsection (d) above and are included in the stated purpose for which the records or communications are sought under subsection (e)(1)(A) above."

(r) Mil. R. Evid. 514(e)(4) is renumbered as Mil. R. Evid. 514(e)(5).

(s) Mil. R. Evid. 514(e)(5) is renumbered as Mil. R. Evid. 514(e)(6).

(t) Mil. R. Evid. 615(e) is amended to read as follows:

"(e) A victim of an offense from the trial of an accused for that offense, unless the military judge, after receiving clear and convincing evidence, determines that testimony by the victim would be materially altered if the victim heard other testimony at that hearing or proceeding."

Sec. <u>3</u>. Part IV of the Manual for Courts-Martial, United States, is amended as follows:

(a) Paragraph 5, Article 81 – Conspiracy, subparagraph a is amended to read as follows:

"a. Text of statute.

(a) Any person subject to this chapter who conspires with any other person to commit an offense under this chapter shall, if one or more of the conspirators does an act to effect the object of the conspiracy, be punished as a court-martial may direct.

(b) Any person subject to this chapter who conspires with any other person to commit an offense under the law of war, and who knowingly performs an overt act to effect the object of the conspiracy, shall be punished, if death results to one or more of the victims, by death or such other punishment as a court-martial or military commission may direct, and, if death does not result to any of the victims, by such punishment, other than death, as a court-martial or military commission may direct."

(b) Paragraph 5, Article 81 – Conspiracy, subparagraph b is amended to read as follows:

"b. *Elements.*

(1) *Conspiracy.*

(a) That the accused entered into an agreement with one or more persons to commit an offense under the UCMJ; and

(b) That, while the agreement continued to exist, and while the accused remained a party to the agreement, the accused or at least one of the co-conspirators performed an overt act for the purpose of bringing about the object of the conspiracy.

(2) *Conspiracy when offense is an offense under the law of war resulting in the death of one or more victims.*

(a) That the accused entered into an agreement with one or more persons to commit an offense under the law of war;

(b) That, while the agreement continued to exist, and while the accused remained a party to the agreement, the accused knowingly performed an overt act for the purpose of bringing about the object of the conspiracy; and

(c) That death resulted to one or more victims."

(c) Paragraph 5, Article 81 – Conspiracy, subparagraph e is amended to read as follows:

"e. *Maximum punishment.* Any person subject to the code who is found guilty of conspiracy shall be subject to the maximum punishment authorized for the offense that is the object of the conspiracy. However, with the exception noted below, if death is an authorized punishment for the offense that is the object of the conspiracy, the maximum punishment shall be dishonorable discharge, forfeiture of all pay and allowances, and confinement for life without eligibility for parole. If the offense that is the object of the conspiracy is an offense under the law of war, the person knowingly performed an overt act for the purpose of bringing about the object of the conspiracy, and death results to one or more victims, the death penalty shall be an available punishment."

(d) Paragraph 5, Article 81 – Conspiracy, subparagraph f is amended to read as follows:

"f. *Sample specifications.*

(1) *Conspiracy.*

In that _____ (personal jurisdiction data), did, (at/on board—location) (subject-matter jurisdiction data, if required), on or about _____ 20 _____, conspire with _____ (and _____) to commit an offense under the Uniform Code of Military Justice, to wit: (larceny of _____ , of a value of (about) $ _____ , the property of _____), and in order to effect the object of the conspiracy the said _____ (and _____) did _____ .

(2) *Conspiracy when offense is an offense under the law of war resulting in the death of one*

or more victims.

In that _____ (personal jurisdiction data), did, (at/on board—location) (subject-matter jurisdiction data, if required), on or about _____ 20 _____, conspire with _____ (and _____) to commit an offense under the law of war, to wit: (murder of _____), and in order to effect the object of the conspiracy the said _____ knowingly did _____ resulting in the death of _____."

(e) Paragraph 16, Article 92 – Failure to obey order or regulation, is amended by inserting after subparagraph b.(3)(c) a new Note and a new subparagraph b.(3)(d) as follows:

"[Note: In cases where the dereliction of duty resulted in death or grievous bodily harm, add the following as applicable]

(d) That such dereliction of duty resulted in death or grievous bodily harm to a person other than the accused."

(f) Paragraph 16, Article 92 – Failure to obey order or regulation, is amended by inserting new subparagraphs c.(3)(e) and (f) immediately after Paragraph 16c.(3)(d) and read as follows:

"(e) Grievous bodily harm. "Grievous bodily harm" means serious bodily injury. It does not include minor injuries, such as a black eye or a bloody nose, but does include fractured or dislocated bones, deep cuts, torn members of the body, serious damage to internal organs, and other serious bodily injuries.

(f) Where the dereliction of duty resulted in death or grievous bodily harm, an intent to cause death or grievous bodily harm is not required."

(g) Paragraph 16, Article 92 – Failure to obey order or regulation, is amended by renumbering the existing subparagraph e.(3)(B) as subparagraph e.(3)(C), inserting new subparagraph e.(3)(B), inserting a new subparagraph e.(3)(D), and inserting a new note following subparagraph e.(3)(D) as follows:

"(B) *Through neglect or culpable inefficiency resulting in death or grievous bodily harm.* Bad-conduct discharge, forfeiture of all pay and allowances, and confinement for 18 months.

(C) *Willful.* Bad-conduct discharge, forfeiture of all pay and allowances, and confinement for 6 months.

(D) *Willful dereliction of duty resulting in death or grievous bodily harm.* Dishonorable discharge, forfeiture of all pay and allowances, and confinement for 2 years."

[Note: For (1) and (2) above, the punishment set forth does not apply in the following cases: if, in the absence of the order or regulation that was violated or not obeyed, the accused would on the same facts be subject to conviction for another specific offense for which a lesser punishment is prescribed; or if the violation or failure to obey is a breach of restraint imposed as a result of an order. In these instances, the maximum punishment is that specifically prescribed elsewhere for that particular offense.]

(h) Paragraph 16, Article 92 – Failure to obey order or regulation, subparagraph f.(4) is amended to read as follows:

"(4) *Dereliction in the performance of duties.*

In that, _____ (personal jurisdiction data), who (knew) (should have known) of his/her duties (at/on board—location) (subject-matter jurisdiction data, if required), (on or about ____ 20__) (from about ____ 20__ to about _____ 20__), was derelict in the performance of those duties in that he/she (negligently) (willfully) (by culpable inefficiency) failed _____, as it was his/her duty to do (, and that such dereliction of duty resulted in (grievous bodily harm, to wit: (broken leg) (deep cut) (fractured skull) to) (the death of) _____)."

(i) Paragraph 17, Article 93 – Cruelty and maltreatment, subparagraph e is amended to read as follows:

" e. *Maximum punishment.* Dishonorable discharge, forfeiture of all pay and allowances, and confinement for 2 years."

(j) Paragraph 57, Article 131 – Perjury, subparagraph c is amended by changing "an investigation conducted under Article 32" to "a preliminary hearing conducted under Article 32" and by changing "an Article 32 investigation" to "an Article 32 preliminary hearing".

(k) Paragraph 96, Article 134 – Obstructing justice, subparagraph f is amended by changing "an investigating officer" to "a preliminary hearing officer" and by changing "before such investigating officer" to "before such preliminary hearing officer."

(l) Paragraph 96a, Article 134 – Wrongful interference with an adverse administrative proceeding, paragraph f is amended by changing "an investigating officer" to "a preliminary hearing officer" and by changing "before such investigating officer" to "before such preliminary hearing officer."

[FR Doc. 2015–15495
Filed 6–19–15; 11:15 am]
Billing code 5000–04

Made in the USA
Lexington, KY
25 May 2017